The
Auschwitz Album

The Auschwitz Album

A Book Based Upon an Album Discovered by a Concentration Camp Survivor, Lili Meier

text by Peter Hellman

Random House · New York

*Grateful acknowledgment is made to the following for permission to reprint previously
published material:*

Beacon Press: Excerpts from *Man's Search for Meaning: An Introduction to Logotherapy* by
Viktor Frankl. Copyright © 1959, 1962 by Viktor Frankl. Reprinted by permission of Beacon Press.

Holocaust Library: Excerpt from *And the Sun Kept Shining* by Bertha Ferderber-Salz,
(1980), pp. 135–136. Reprinted by permission of Holocaust Library.

Routledge and Kegan Paul Ltd. and Stein and Day Publishers: Excerpt from *Auschwitz
Inferno* (British title) and *Eyewitness Auschwitz* (American title) by Filip Muller. Copyright ©
1979 by Filip Muller. Translation Copyright © 1979 by Routledge & Kegan Paul Ltd.
Reprinted by permission of Routledge & Kegan Paul Ltd. and Stein and Day Publishers.

Sidgwick & Jackson Ltd., Publishers: Excerpt from *I Cannot Forgive* by Rudolf Vrba.
Reprinted by permission of Sidgwick & Jackson Ltd. and Anthony Gibbs & Phillips (as
co-publishers).

Times Books and Penguin Books: Excerpt from *Anus Mundi: The 1500 Days in Auschwitz/
Birkenau* by Wieslaw Kielar. Copyright © 1979 by Wieslaw Kielar and S. Fischer Verlag
GmbH, Frankfurt am Main. Reprinted by permission of Times Books, a division of Quadrangle/The New York Times Book Co., Inc., and Penguin Books.

Twayne Publishers: Excerpt from *Hope Is the Last to Die* by Halina Birenbaum. Copyright
© 1971 by Halina Birenbaum. Reprinted by permission of Twayne Publishers, A Division
of G. K. Hall & Co., Boston.

Vallentine, Mitchell & Co., Ltd.: Excerpts from *Journey Through Hell* by Reska Weiss
(1961). Reprinted by permission of Vallentine, Mitchell & Co., Ltd., London.

Library of Congress Cataloging in Publication Data
Main entry under title:
The Auschwitz album.
1. Oświęcim (Concentration camp)—Pictorial works.
2. Holocaust, Jewish (1938–1945)—Pictorial works.
I. Hellman, Peter.   II. Meier, Lili, 1926–
III. Klarsfeld, Beate.
D805.P7A93   943.086   80-53907
ISBN 0-394-51932-9

Manufactured in the United States of America
24689753
First Edition

Design by Bernard Klein

223467

17.77   11-10-82

AUTHOR'S NOTE

Peter Hellman thanks the following persons for their counsel in the preparation of this book: Dina Abramowicz, Moshe Avital (who graciously allowed use of his unpublished history of Jewish life in Bilke), Randolph Braham, Tzipora Hager Halivni, Raul Hilberg, Cyma Horowitz, Isador Reisman, Naftali Weisz.

Introduction

ON the night of May 24, 1944, a train of forty-five boxcars left the siding of the brick factory that served as a transit ghetto in the Carpathian city of Berehovo. Of the 3,500 Hungarian Jews on board, one contingent was from Bilke, a town in the hills twenty-five miles away. It included the family of eighteen-year-old Lili Jacob, who, one year later, would find the album of photos reproduced here. As was customary in the deportations, passage for all those aboard was paid for by the SS, the price being computed on the number of kilometers to the destination.

The train threaded through the northern hills of the Carpathian range, then headed west. At Kassa the Hungarian police guards on board were relieved by SS men. After a day and a half, the train passed through the ancient Polish royal city of Cracow. Here, in response to the entreaties from within, a bucket of water was passed into each boxcar. Then the train continued west for thirty-five miles to the small, previously unremarkable city that the Poles call Oświęcim and the Germans called—and would teach the world to call—Auschwitz.

The concentration camp on the edge of the city, known as Auschwitz I, or the main camp, was not, as is commonly thought, where some two million Jews were sent to be killed; the single, small gas-chamber crematorium at the northwestern corner of the camp would not have been equal to that task. Auschwitz I had been established on the site of an old army garrison to imprison Polish political prisoners of the Nazis. Though Jews with useful skills did come to be incarcerated here, along with non-Jews of many nationalities, they were always in the minority. In any case, the inscription wrought in iron over the main gate, "Work Shall Make You Free," was never meant to apply to the Jews—though they had little to hope for except that it might be so.

The killing center, largest and most efficient of those established on Polish soil by the Nazis, was known as Auschwitz II, or Birkenau. It had been built a mile and a half west of Auschwitz I at Himmler's order following his visit in March 1941. Birkenau was operational late in the following winter, when it received Russian prisoners of war as well as Jews. At first there was no rail line to

Birkenau. Arriving deportees had to be unloaded at a special ramp ("Judenramp") midway between the two camps and then marched or trucked the rest of the way to Birkenau. That had been the method for nearly two and a half years. But in anticipation of the large and hurried influx of Hungarian Jews planned for the spring of 1944, a faster method of delivering people into the camp was needed. By May 15, 1944—target date for the first deportation of Carpathian Jews—a new rail spur leading directly into Birkenau was complete.

On the morning of May 26 the train from Berehovo rolled off the main line onto this new spur. Almost at once the land turned swampy and all signs of settlement disappeared. Those who were able to peer out of the small, high barred windows of the boxcars could see, rising out of this muddy isolation, a low and vast gray compound of huts behind high fences and guard towers. Somewhat off center, on the southeast side, was a high arch over which rose the main watchtower of the camp. The train passed beneath this arch into a sealed kingdom from which the barest few—Lili Jacob, alone from her large family was one—would return.

The fate of these Jews was meant to be concealed—particularly from the world outside. Therefore, as a rule, photographing the prisoners at Birkenau was strictly forbidden. Brazen as they were, the Nazis seem to have known it would be wiser if no record were made of their crime here or at the other killing centers. And so, during the first two and a half years of deportations to Birkenau the trains arrived day and night, delivering more than a million Jews to this place, yet not one photo is known to have been made of them.

That is why it was so remarkable that when the doors of this transport from Berehovo were at last unlocked, there was, in addition to the normal SS "reception" team, an SS man standing on the ramp holding not the usual pistol or cane, but instead a camera at the ready. It is not known who this photographer was, or who authorized him to photograph freely on the ramp, or for what purpose this exception to the rule had been granted. Neither is it known on how many other days, during the seven weeks of the Hungarian deportations, he also made photos for this album. But judging from the thoroughness and one might even say the sensitivity with which he did his job, it does seem as if the photographer understood that his assignment was unique—that he alone would record on film the faces of the people delivered to Birkenau for martyrdom.

The first snap of the shutter apparently occurred even before the doors of the boxcar were opened and as the SS men scurried to their stations. The next pictures show the dazed occupants tumbling out of the cars. Then, as they were herded into long ragged columns, five across—one for men and the other for women and young children—the photographer moved among them, sometimes snapping a hundred faces at once, sometimes a single face. He did not neglect the beautiful child or the bent grandmother, the crippled or the evidently retarded.

The photographer was at the head of these columns where the selection took place. Up to this point, families could stay more or less abreast of one another in the two columns. Whatever miseries and cruelties they had endured, they had at least endured them together. But now, with a casual flick of his finger, the tall SS selector would finally and irreparably splinter them apart. Those selected for work went right, those selected for immediate gassing went left. When Lili Jacob, the teen-ager from Bilke, was sent to the right, she impulsively ran back to her mother and her two youngest brothers, who had been sent to the left. For this act a guard stabbed her in the arm. It is doubtful that the photographer would have recorded this incident even if he had been in position to do so. In keeping with the innocent-seeming title of the album that Lili Jacob found—"Resettlement of Hungarian Jews"—he seems to have avoided recording acts of violence.

The photographer did some of his work from atop the boxcars. From there he could record the unobstructed vista of the milling about, the long columns of people, the attending prisoners in their striped uniforms, the trucks hauling away luggage, the occasional old woman or infant adrift and confused amid the towering, strutting SS men, canes in hand to poke those who did not respond quickly enough to orders that were barked out in a language most of the deportees could not understand.

Pointed to the south, the camera caught the great portal of the main watchtower looming against a gray sky. Swung around to the north, at the head of the tracks, the camera picked up two large buildings with high smokestacks—the most substantial structures in the sprawling complex. These were crematoria I and II. Extending in an ell from them, but hidden underground, were the dressing rooms and the gas chambers. These were the most efficient killing facilities ever designed.

Following the selection, the photographer left the ramp and headed into the depths of the camp to record each group according to its fate. He followed, separately, the glum-faced columns of "able-bodied" men and women selected to be slaves, showing them as they are marched off for processing. He followed those considered unfit for work—women with small children, the ill and the elderly. They had been told they were going to the "delousing" station, after which they would be admitted to the "family camp." There, they were assured, they would find the luggage that had been taken from them. There, also, they could look forward to visits from the working members of their families.

Along a route defined by electrified fences, the photographer followed this last group until it reached a wooded area at the western periphery of the camp. This place was known as the *Birkenau*—the birch alley—which gave its name to the entire camp. Here, amid pines and birches, he photographed the people as they waited. These trees, spindly though they were, helped to obscure the sight lines to other killing facilities located farther back in the grove. Clinging to their hopes and to every word of blandishment offered to them by their SS escort, these people walked on trustingly to their fate. Even when, in one startling photograph (#126), a group of seemingly calm women and children pass directly in front and in full view of such a facility, it is clear that they have no idea of what it is or that this is their own last hour on earth.

The photographer also visited the compound where trucks and wagons arrived from the ramp with the confiscated suitcases, trunks, briefcases, bundles, baskets, water bottles and kitchen utensils. To this property would be added the clothing and personal items left behind in the dressing rooms of the gas chambers and at the "sauna" where those selected for slave labor would likewise be stripped. Here, under especially watchful SS eyes, the booty was sorted into great heaps. The best of it would be shipped back to the Reich. This compound, as well as the brigade assigned to work here, was called "Canada" because it was filled with riches.

FROM the late winter of 1942 through the fall of 1944, more than one million Jews arrived at Birkenau. Many, like the family of Lili Jacob, brought with them, as part of their fifty-kilogram baggage allotment, not only the practical necessities of life, but also their treasured family photographs. Who knew, after all, whether they might be separated from one another, and if so for how long? All such pictures, useless to their captors, were destroyed. In their place we have only the 185 photographs taken by the SS and now published here. They alone must stand as the visual record of those who were obliterated.

Such a record might not exist if the album containing these photographs had not been discovered at a German camp called Dora upon its liberation by the Americans on April 11, 1945. That camp, deep within the Reich, was five hundred miles from Birkenau. And that date was five months after the dismantling and dynamiting of Birkenau's four main killing facilities before the arrival of the advancing Russians.

That Lili Jacob discovered the album is extraordinary when one considers that out of hundreds of thousands of families who arrived unrecorded at Birkenau from countless villages and towns, it was people from her community and even members of her family that were among those photographed within.

LILI Jacob was born on January 16, 1926, in a house on the main street of Bilke. It was a beautiful little town, set in a valley deep in the mountains. No fewer than six streams and rivers rushed down from the heavily forested hills. The story is told that centuries ago, a local nobleman's daughter drowned while bathing in the widest of these rivers, and the grieving father gave her name both to the river and to the settlement.

The beauty of the city helped neither Jew nor Christian to escape the general poverty that prevailed in the region, known by the unwieldy name of Sub-Carpathian Ruthenia. A study of social conditions made in 1921 indicated that nearly one half of the Jews there had no means of employment. Even by pre-war standards, conditions were primitive as well as impoverished. Half a century after electric lights had come to Budapest, Bilke still had none. The only telephones in town were at the police station and the post office.

The range of mountains in which Bilke was located served as a buffer as well as a bridge between two worlds. To the east was Russia; to the west was Middle Europe. Here, in between, sparks flew off the edges of both. Until World War I, this had been the eastern territory of the Austro-Hungarian Empire, governed with a mixture of disinterest and dishonesty from Budapest. Upon the dissolution of the Empire in 1918, the region was accorded to the newly assembled nation of Czechoslovakia. The new government ruling from Prague was progressive but short-lived.

As Hitler dismembered the Czechoslovak republic two decades later, he threw scraps to those nations whose help he might need. To Hungary he offered, among other items, this part of the Carpathians. The offer was quickly accepted. This did not sit well with the local Ukrainian nationalists, who, on March 13, 1939, declared an independent Ruthenian republic. Under immediate Hungarian attack, the republic lasted only one day. Once again, the region answered to Budapest. At the next division of spoils, in 1945, the territory was taken by the Soviets as a province of their own.

All these political transmutations were being visited on anything but a homogeneous populace. Among the ten thousand residents of Bilke were Ukrainians, Jews, Ruthenians, Poles, Germans, Hungarians and Czechs. As a result, the place was a crazy quilt of languages. In Lili Jacob's house, for example, Yiddish was usually spoken. But when her parents didn't want their children to understand, they conversed in Hungarian—the language in which *they* had been schooled. Lili herself attended a public school, where she spoke Czech. At her religious school she learned the Hebrew of the Bible. In the streets and at market she spoke to the peasants in Ruthenian, the ancient dialect of the peasants.

The Jews of Bilke then numbered some two hundred families. Their simple homes of brick or stone were spread along or near the main road, well mixed among those of their Christian neighbors.

There had never been a ghetto, enforced or otherwise, in Bilke. Typically, even the poorest families had at least a small garden in which grew an array of flowers, vegetables and grapes, as well as fruit and nut trees. There was a large synagogue, known as the *grosse shul,* and several smaller places of worship. Everyone in the community knew everyone else. In the Yiddish phrase of Lili's Aunt Margit, they were *geknipt und gebinden*—knotted and pasted.

No family in Bilke was considered to be poor as long as it could manage to set a proper Sabbath table. Lili was up with her mother at two o'clock each Friday morning to bake the traditional cakes and bread. From then on the cooking and cleaning proceeded through the afternoon. One hour before sunset the younger children brought the following day's noon meal in a pot, called *cholent,* to the communal oven in the synagogue courtyard. When all pots were accounted for, the sexton, David Reisman, walled up the front of the oven with iron planks and sealed it with wet clay.

A few moments before sunset each family assembled at the Sabbath table to watch the mother light the candles and, hands covering eyes, sing the blessing that welcomed the Sabbath as "queen of days." It was traditional in Bilke to light a candle for each member of the family. With big families the norm, that meant a splendid blaze. Isador Reisman, one of eight children of the sexton, remembers how he closed his eyes as his mother intoned the blessing—not all the way, but just enough for his eyelashes to mesh and make the candle flames burst into stars.

After the candle lighting, the men gathered in the big and small synagogues to pray. Bilke was not a place where Sabbath prayers were mumbled quickly. Yoheshuah Doft, cantor of the community, sang the prayers assisted by a choir of his six sons. He was known for a strong tenor that could break suddenly to a keening falsetto, and his sons for the sweet interplay of their voices. These prayers were sent up from a synagogue that was high-ceilinged and airy, with a frieze of biblical scenes painted overhead. Graceful candelabra provided soft light from above. In the season of the spring holiday of Shavuot, the synagogue was decked out with fresh cuttings of greens.

By seven o'clock the men were hurrying home. At the Sabbath table each householder raised the ceremonial cup and, in this region famous for its wines, blessed the fruit of the vine. He cut and blessed the challah, the braided bread, which had been covered with a white cloth so as "not to be embarrassed" that the wine had been blessed first. Then all dined on the traditional foods—fish, chicken soup, beef brisket if the family could afford it, noodle pudding, stewed fruits, and the cakes baked in the dark of that morning. At the table of Naftali Svi Weiss, chief rabbi of the community and head of the city's renowned yeshivah, eating and discussing scripture were combined into an art both subtle and regulated.

On Saturday morning the men were back in the synagogue at nine o'clock. After services concluded three hours later, the sexton broke open the seal on the communal oven, and with a long-handled spatula, drew out each family's pot for the noonday meal. Even in winter snows they would be too hot to touch, and the children who brought the pots home carried them with mittens. The afternoons were given over to naps and visiting. Lili walked with her family for forty-five minutes to visit her maternal grandparents, who lived on a small farm on a hillside outside town. "It was what I looked forward to all week," she says. "For us, the family was the whole thing."

Most of the local Jews traced their roots back to Galicia or the Ukraine, from which they had fled a succession of pogroms commencing with those of Bogdan Chmelnitsky in the seventeenth century. But Lili's maternal grandparents had come from Turkey, and her paternal grandparents from Palestine. Her father was a horse trader who traveled to neighboring cities for the livestock markets that were regularly held. In many parts of Europe this would have been considered to be an unusual occupation for a Jew, but in the Carpathians it was normal. Bernard Bergman, a Polish-born Jew, remembers a train ride through the region in 1938 during which he struck up a conversation with another Jew in Yiddish. Bergman asked about his profession.

"I am a businessman," the man answered.

"What business?"

"I drive cattle from town to town" came the forthright reply.

Bergman thought that was funny, and still does. To him, an urban Jew, this was not a businessman; it was a Jewish cowboy. But in a region where nearly everyone was tied to the land, "businessman" was a relative term.

As the eldest of six children and the only girl, Lili grew up treated like a princess. She also admits to having been "nosy." Not a wedding or funeral occurred in Bilke that she missed. She would slip in behind the celebrants as easily at one of the town churches as at the synagogue. She knew of every romance, every scandal. Bilke was the perfect size for a girl like her. She never had to miss a thing. There survives but a single photo in which Lili appears as a child, and it seems to confirm her own view of herself from the time. It is not a portrait of her immediate family but that of her Aunt Margit. It is meant to be a photo only of them, but in the extreme foreground is a small face, smiling impishly, as if she had popped into the photo unannounced and uninvited as the shutter snapped.

Lili was a good student for a child of little patience. Her mother had hoped to turn her into a dressmaker. Lili readily agreed to take a class with a local woman, chiefly because it allowed her to be out in the evenings later than she would otherwise be permitted. But she barely learned to turn a hem. She ended up doing what she much preferred—traveling by bus and occasionally by train to nearby towns to deliver dresses to clients of her teacher. She sought out every opportunity, as well, to deliver registration papers to customers who had bought horses from her father. Best of all, she looked forward to occasions when he would invite her to join him on the last day of a market in one of the provincial cities. "It seems silly," she says, "but my most vivid memory is of a salad we ate together in a restaurant in Chust—so fresh, so filled with good things…"

RELATIONS between Jews and Christians were decent enough in Bilke. Tolerance was further encouraged during the two decades of progressive Czechoslovak rule between the wars. Neighbors helped one another, regardless of religion, and even socialized. Lili's own best friend was the daughter of the local police constable, a Christian. While intermarriage in Prague and Budapest was common, it was known to have happened in the three-hundred-year-old Jewish community of Bilke exactly once. In 1933 a Jewish farm girl from an outlying part of town insisted on marrying the Christian boy from the farm across the road. All the tears and threats in Bilke could not dissuade her. With her vows, she was banished from the Jewish community as well as from her family. Lili remembers, as a young girl, visiting the home of the girl's parents, who were carrying out the rite of mourning, exactly as if the bride had died.

An odd and unsettling presentiment of the future was felt in Bilke during Easter week of 1935. By custom of the Christian townspeople, it was said that during that week, the bells of the Ukrainian Catholic church—or, at least, their ringing—had "flown" to Rome. And so, they were silent. This was the sort of tradition well understood by the Jews, who had no lack of such customs of their own.

One morning during that Easter week a young Jewish man who was so mentally deranged that he had to be kept chained at home broke loose and disappeared. As his family and others from the community searched for him, the church bells abruptly rang out—not prettily, but in wild tintinnabulation. From every quarter of Bilke, people ran to see what had happened. The Christians were enraged to discover that a Jew was in the bell tower. Deranged or not, he had profaned their Holy Week. The crowd separated into groups of Christians and Jews. Silently they faced each other, the age-old hostilities and mutual fears suddenly to the fore. Only the arrival of the police prevented violence. As Lili's Aunt Margit said, "Things were nice on the surface, but they could never forgive us for killing Jesus."

THE Jews of Bilke understood that the rise of Hitler would bring nothing good to them or to any of their people. But the Reich was distant, and in any case, what would anyone gain by persecuting people as poor as they? Even when Hitler took the Sudetenland, put Bohemia and Moravia under his "protection," and made a puppet republic out of Slovakia, they felt sure that his hand would never reach them in Bilke, where, as Moshe Avital, youngest son of the cantor, says, "the surrounding forests were so thick that it seemed the beginnings of time were hidden in them."

The first direct blow to the community came one evening in March 1939. It was then that Hungarian troops moved, at Hitler's invitation, to take over this portion of the Carpathian region and to quickly subdue the uprising of the local Ukrainian nationalists. Bilke, in particular, was a hotbed of this movement. In the synagogue that night, the Jews finished praying and hurried home in advance of the nine o'clock curfew that had been announced for the town. Among them was the cobbler Benjamin Klein, an officer of the synagogue and of the cooperative burial society. His piety and charity were well known. Between blows of his hammer in his shop, he would sing out words of Scripture and sayings of the sages. He welcomed destitute wanderers—there were many in the Carpathians—to stay at his home. It was said, in fact, that his house was situated at the edge of Bilke so that wanderers would see it first. That very evening, he had collected a few coins in the synagogue to give to a destitute man who had arrived earlier in the day.

On the bridge over the first stream, as Klein dashed home, shots were fired. One hit him in the head. When he was carried home by other congregants, his family assumed at first that they were bringing another helpless stranger whom Klein had agreed to care for. Benjamin Klein died before the doctor could come. Still in his hand were the coins of charity he had collected at the synagogue.

The next blow, coming in 1941, was an order of deportation for all persons who could not certify their Hungarian citizenship. This order was aimed primarily at the many Jews who had recently fled from untenable conditions in Poland in the 1930s. But many other Jews, epecially in poor and primitive regions like the Carpathians, had lived in the same homes for a generation or more without securing the correct papers (a bribe was often required). In Bilke, two dozen such families were given twenty-four hours' notice to leave their homes. In all, 18,000 suddenly stateless Jews from this region were pushed across the Polish border, where they fell into the hands of the SS. On August 27–28, at Kamanets Podolsk, they were shot and buried in mass graves.

Though Hungary was fascist and allied to Nazi Germany, it remained, for the time being, an independent nation. Legally, Hitler could not make the government of the aged regent, Admiral Miklos Horthy, do anything. It cannot be said that Horthy's enthusiasm for doing in the Jews approached Hitler's, but under Nazi prodding, the usual anti-Jewish measures were implemented in Hungary, just as they were in nations that had been physically occupied. Jews were defined by bloodline and had to register. They were banished from the professions, trades and schools. Their businesses and assets were confiscated. Still, for a while, the Hungarian Jews were spared from the ultimate measure. They were not deported.

These anti-Jewish measures hit hard in the Jacob home. Martin Jacob's license to deal in horses was withdrawn and he was without income. Lili was banned from entering high school. Gradually, food supplies dwindled. By the spring of 1943 Lili had decided she could no longer be idle. Instead of languishing at home, she would go, after the Passover holiday, to Budapest and find work to help her family. Her father's reaction was predictable: "He almost grabbed a knife and cut my throat."

Most seventeen-year-old girls would have backed down. But Lili's determination was unwavering, and it was not she but her father who backed down. Immediately after the festival of Shavout, she went to Budapest and on the same day found a job at a Jewish orphanage. Many of the children received at this place were not actually orphans but had been left there by parents who had fled from Slovakia and other areas from which Jews were already being deported. The parents often remained nearby, hiding with false papers. Regularly, Lili saw them gazing through the fence at their children playing in the orphanage yard. It was drilled into the children never to say they had parents, never to reveal where they had lived before. As long as the origins of these children remained unknown, the Hungarian authorities allowed them to remain safe from deportation.

In the early spring of 1944 Hitler abruptly ended his arm's-length dealing with the Hungarian government—particularly on the "Jewish question." On March 18 he lured Horthy to a meeting at Schloss Klessheim and did not let him go home. That night Nazi troops occupied Hungary. A few days later the master technician of the "final solution," Adolf Eichmann, arrived in Budapest with his team of seasoned deportation specialists. It had been almost a year since Lili's own arrival, and she sensed that the worst was near. Friends advised her to get false papers and stay in Budapest, where it was easier to get "lost." Among them was Izzy, her boyfriend from back home, who was planning to do the same thing himself. But Lili never even considered it. Whatever was coming, she would suffer with her family. She got on the train and went home to await the worst.

She found her five brothers wearing clothing with "patches on patches." Her father, previously an ebullient man, was withdrawn and quiet. Her mother remained cheerful, even though there was less than ever to put on the table. In spite of all this, Lili found herself happy. "We were together," she explained. "That was my happiness." As Passover approached, Lili and her mother sewed the newly required yellow star on the family clothing.

Passover is a holiday more bound up in custom and ritual than any other on the Jewish calendar. Despite the oppressive times, the community in Bilke tried to celebrate it in 1944 just as they always had. Late in the winter those who could still afford it had rendered the fat of specially fed chickens and geese to be put up in jars for the Passover cooking. Officials of the synagogue rented a mill where, after the stone wheel was purified with hot coals and the premises blessed by the rabbi, grain was ground into flour for matzoh. Women cleaned and recleaned their houses and unwrapped the holiday kitchenware and dinnerware. At each Seder table the story of the Exodus was told through symbol, question and song. On this Passover of 1944 the traditional words of the service had never seemed so piercing:

"This year a slave, next year a free man....Next year in Jerusalem!"

But even as this hope was announced in early March, the tracks of the Birkenau rail spur had, in anticipation of the arrival of these very people, reached to the gates of the gas chambers–crematoria.

Well after midnight at the end of the eighth and last day of Passover, there was a thump on the Jacob door. Lili and her mother, as it happened, were up baking bread for the new week. Cracking the door open fearfully, they found a notable of the Jewish community who had just come from a meeting called by the local police. His message was to the point: "Bake extra bread. Tomorrow we are to be taken away for resettlement on farms in Poland."

At first light, Lili went out with her mother to a corner of the garden. There Mrs. Jacob buried her wedding ring and a pair of fine earrings given to her by her husband. Then they went back inside to pack—no more than fifty kilograms per person, by police order. What to bring to the "farm camps"? Durable clothing, blankets, rolled mattresses, essential toiletries and kitchen utensils, prayer books. The rest, including furniture, would go on loan to the neighbors.

Under Hungarian police escort the Jews of Bilke assembled at midmorning in the courtyard of the *grosse shul.* Since the war began, their numbers had diminished markedly. There had been the two dozen families who had been deported in 1941. Many others had fled to Budapest, where they had done what Lili rejected—arranged for false papers and tried to blend in. A few, especially in outlying areas, escaped into the forest. Nearly all the young men were gone, having been drafted into the Hungarian Labor Service, an auxiliary to the regular army that dug trenches at the front, cleared mine-fields, built roads, airstrips and bridges. They had suffered heavy casualties, and sometimes it was not Russians but their own army commanders who killed them. And so the community stood—barely 1,500 in all. The hand of Hitler, which they had believed would never reach Bilke, had them in its grip.

In the afternoon the community was loaded onto a train. On the outskirts of Berehovo, the train stopped beside the brick factory that was to be the transit ghetto. The people were lodged in the open sheds where bricks normally dried. Organizing themselves quickly, they partitioned the sheds into cubicles by hanging blankets. Each family had only enough space to lie down. With Jews arriving by the hour from the surrounding villages, as well as from Berehovo itself, the fenced-in and guarded population of the brick factory soon stood at 10,000.

Berehovo was one of thirteen cities in Sub-Carpathian Ruthenia where, in the days following Passover of 1944, ghettos for nearly 300,000 Jews were established. Their leaders had been assured that they would shortly be resettled in labor camps in Poland. The truth was that ghettoization was the first step in an elaborate plan laid out by Adolf Eichmann and his team in Budapest. They had divided

Hungary into six zones from which deportations would occur according to a precisely phased schedule. Sub-Carpathian Ruthenia was Zone One.

On April 19, 1944, the Bilke contingent in the Berehovo ghetto received an unexpected visitor. He was Isador Reisman, the sexton's son, now eighteen years old and a member of a labor brigade billeted in Budapest. He had been granted an overnight pass; in retrospect, he believes the pass was granted not so much as an act of good will as a ploy to make the people think things were "fairly normal."

Reisman was stunned and saddened to see how the people—especially the elderly—had to live in the open, still-chill spring air, without comforts or food except what they had brought. But he was also filled with admiration at their "lack of panic and their persisting faith." That night Reisman slept on the ground in his family's cubicle, awakening in the morning to the hum of prayers asking for deliverance. His father had brought a small tool chest from home, at the bottom of which he kept a Bible. Reisman listened to him recite a Psalm of David: "I lift up my eyes to the hills. From whence does my help come?..."

"As he recited this verse," says Reisman, "he looked up at the hills around Berehovo, which were covered with vineyards and very beautiful. And it was true that on the other side of those hills was the Red Army, advancing steadily. But they would arrive too late to save those people."

When Reisman left the ghetto to report back to his unit, a slow-moving train stopped at the gate. The only two passengers to get off were an elderly couple from Bilke, Fishl Jesovic and his paralyzed wife. At first he had been allowed to stay behind with her. Now he had been required to bring her on a bed. The last to arrive, a few days later, were Yitzhok Davidowitz and his wife, who had been nearing the full term of pregnancy. She also had been permitted to remain in Bilke until her delivery. The infant had died. Seeing the conditions in the ghetto, Davidowitz was heard to say that perhaps the baby had "chosen well."

As the train carrying Reisman back to his unit in Budapest passed by the ghetto, children standing behind the fence waved. Reisman saw that he was the only one waving back. "I looked away then," he says, "and my heart broke." Weeks later he got a last postcard from his mother:

My sweet son:
They have herded us together. They are taking us away
—where, we don't know. We hope for the best. We
are in God's hands. You take care of yourself.
With love,
your mother, Roza

THE Berehovo ghetto was emptied in four transports of about 2,500 persons each. The first left on May 19, and the last about ten days later. The elderly were, for the most part, held back until the others had been removed.

With her sojourn in Budapest behind her, Lili considered herself to be an adult woman. But in the dark and crowded boxcar of the deportation train as it pulled away from Berehovo, she suddenly found herself weeping loudly. Her mother took her daughter's head in her lap then, and as when she was an infant, smoothed and stroked her hair gently, saying, "Don't worry, honey. Because you came home, we are together."

Two and a half days later, on the Birkenau ramp, Lili was ripped away from her mother and the rest of the family. That last moment they were together is still marked, to the precise moment, by the angry scar on the arm of the Jacob family's sole survivor.

At the "sauna" Lili gave up her clothing, a pair of gold earrings she had been given for her thirteenth birthday, and a watch. After processing she was given a rag of a blue dress marked on the back with a stripe of white paint. Then her group was marched off to compund B IIc, known as the Hungarian women's camp. After hours of standing at attention in front of the kitchen, Lili and several hundred other women were taken to hut 16. They were kept there until compound B IIb, the Czech "family" camp, was emptied by the murder of its last 9,000 inhabitants. On July 25, Lili was tattooed on the left arm. Her number, in one of two new series begun that spring, was A-10862.

Lili was assigned to a team of several strong women who, like beasts of burden, pulled a wagon into which they emptied the latrines as well as the night buckets kept at the back of each hut. This work detail was known as the *Scheisskommando,* and it was said that, especially on a hot day, one and all, oppressed and oppressor, ran from their path. This was not quite true, since SS guards, whatever the weather, stayed close enough to beat the women constantly with their rifle butts. Lili sustained permanent damage to her back from those blows.

The women pulled the loaded wagons out to the fields to be dumped for fertilizer. On one of these runs, in a death-defying act, a prisoner tossed Lili a potato he had just pulled from the ground. Lili slipped it into her dress in an instant. That night she did not eat her ration of black bread but wrapped it around the potato. It "slow-cooked" under her body as she slept and she took care not to roll over. In the morning the potato had softened. Even today, when she thinks about how she ate that "sandwich," her face lights into a blazing smile.

Lili wore her blue dress all that spring, summer and fall. The cold weather came and still she had nothing else to wear. Finally she was given a navy-blue wool coat from the ample stock available in "Canada" at the end of a year of unprecedented gassings. Then, in December, she was shipped off to the west, away from the advancing Russian armies. She was put to work at one labor camp after another until she finally came to Dora, a satellite of the underground missile works at Nordhausen, Germany. By then it was early April 1945. Many prisoners who had survived everything else could not make it through that last winter of the war. Even Lili, despite her formidable strength and will, yielded to typhus.

In the clinic for prisoners she remembers being observed, along with two other cases, by a prisoner-doctor who, thinking none of them could understand, said to a colleague in Czech, "This one we can save." He pointed to Lili, who then weighed only eighty pounds.

"For the gas?" she shot back in Czech from her stretcher, still finding the strength for sarcasm.

Just a few days later, lying half asleep, Lili was suddenly aware of confusion all around her. SS men flew in every direction. And then she heard shouts: "The Americans are here!" Lili got up and went out to see for herself but she did not get very far before collapsing. Fellow prisoners carried her to a newly vacated SS barrack and put her on a bed. She awoke after about an hour, groggy and cold. Reaching into a cupboard beside the bed, she found a pajama top. Underneath it lay a brown cloth-bound album, frayed at the corners. At that moment Lili cared only about putting on the pajama top and going back to sleep. Awakening later, she felt better. Her curiosity revived, she took the album from the cupboard and opened it.

Thousands of trains had come to Auschwitz-Birkenau. A million people, perhaps even more, had been murdered there. Out of all those transports, and all those people, Lili found herself gazing, on the very first page of the album, at the face of Naftali Svi Weiss, her own rabbi from Bilke. Mesmerized, she turned the pages to discover the faces of other members of her community and even of her own family.

Lili was weak—not only from typhus but from malnutrition and its complications. But she was not so weak that, despite the best efforts of several American officers, she could be made to give up the Auschwitz Album. To her it was not a question of pride in being the discoverer of a unique historical document—it was too early for anyone to evaluate the book as that. For Lili, it was a matter of holding on to a strange yet authentic family album in lieu of a real family. Besides, she did not believe that chance had brought the album to her: it had been an act of Providence. If and when the time should ever come to give it up, Providence would also arrange for that moment. In the interim, she would hold tight to it.

A month later, when she had recovered sufficient strength, Lili headed eastward through Russian-held territory toward home. At a security checkpoint, some soldiers took the album from her, as the Americans had not, by physical force. For three hours they held it—but Lili "shrieked" so much that finally they gave it back. When she arrived back in Bilke in midsummer 1945, the album was all that she carried with her.

Lili had not come home to grieve. She had come only hoping to find someone else from the family who had survived. But there was no one. Even the family home was occupied by squatters. It took the intercession of officials who had known her family to get it back. She quickly discovered, however, that she did not want it back. "To sleep in that place," she says, "alone, by myself, was a horror."

Each morning she went to the train station to see if, by some miracle, anyone from the family had finally come home. She waited each day, all day. She was a bit startled to be joined, from time to time, by the Christian man whose marriage to a Jewish woman had caused such consternation in Bilke. Esther had been married in the church, her four children had been baptized and raised as Christians. She herself had been cast out of the Jewish community. But none of that mattered. She and her children had been deported with the other Jews. None of them came back, just as nobody else from Lili's family came back.

One who did come home was her old boyfriend, Izzy. He had survived, as he had tried to persuade Lili to do, with false papers in Budapest. She was happy to find him alive, and she did not resist his proposal for a quick marriage. Was there anything else to consider? The neighbors kindly set about arranging the wedding which neither set of parents was there to provide. Lili was aware that her own parents had not approved of Izzy, and they had not hidden their feelings from him. Then, barely a week before the date of the wedding, a blissfully smiling Izzy said to Lili, "I'm so happy. Now nobody can stop us from doing what we want to do."

Lili felt herself stiffen. "It was as if he was saying," she explains, "that it was a good thing for us that our parents had died."

The next day, a Sunday, Max Zelmonovic came to visit. He was from a family that had been friendly with hers. He had grown up in Mukachevo. Though he was seven years older than she, Lili remembered that as a girl she had thought him to be quite handsome. But once, during a visit to her father, he had playfully given her a pinch on the cheek. When she protested, he only laughed.

"How I hated him for that," says Lili. Then she had been thirteen and he twenty. Now, when she was nineteen and he twenty-six, Max asked her to come with him to Mukachevo, where he had just opened a small restaurant. She was packed in an hour. "It wasn't hard to leave," she explains, "because I wasn't leaving anything."

Lili worked long hours with Max at the restaurant. He was anxious to get married, but Lili, though happy with him, was not happy with Mukachevo. According to the redrawn border of 1945, this was now Soviet territory, and as she succinctly puts it, "I'd had Nazism, and I didn't need Communism." Now a childhood aspiration revived: she wanted to emigrate to America. Max preferred at first to remain in Mukachevo, but when the authorities proposed putting the restaurant under public ownership with Max as manager, he changed his mind.

They used what little money they had saved to bribe their way across the border into Czechoslovakia, where Max first worked on a farm and then in a factory. They were married on November 26, 1945. The ring Max slipped on Lili's finger was her mother's, dug up from the garden at home. The coat she wore was the same one issued to her at Birkenau. As a survivor, she was glad and proud to wear the garment of another Jewish woman deportee to Birkenau whose name and fate were unknown.

The couple continued to live in penury, especially after the birth of a daughter, Esther, in December, 1946. Lili knew, however, that in the Auschwitz Album she had something of value. Already, by word of mouth alone, its existence had become quickly and widely known. In Bilke, and then in Mukachevo, survivors had appeared, asking if they could look through its pages for lost relatives. On the few occasions when somebody did spot a loved one, Lili gladly gave them the photo.

At the suggestion of Rabbi Bernard Farkas, formerly of Mukachevo and then living in the Bohemian city of Bodmocli-Deczin, Lili took her album to officials of the Jewish Council in Prague. They were eager to buy it for the Jewish Museum there, but Lili would not part with it. She did, however, allow the photos to be copied on glass plates for a payment of 10,000 crowns. With that money and the sponsorship of a distant relative of Max's in New York, they were able to go to America. The passport picture of Lili from that time shows a pretty, soft, even dreamy face that looks as if it had never known a moment of suffering.

LILI and Max arrived in New York on November 1, 1948. A month later they went on to Miami, where they had been advised that job opportunities were good. They knew nobody, but for two people from the Carpathian range, this environment seemed a wonderland. Under the sponsorship of HIAS, a Jewish social service agency, Max was enrolled in a training program for butchers, at the end of which he found work at a local market.

Lili received a jolt from an unexpected quarter when, after nearly a year in a single rented room, she and Max were looking for their first real apartment. One evening they happened to see a modest building with a vacancy sign posted. Inside, the couple chatted with the landlady and her friend, both emigrant Jews themselves. Then, as she and Max were leaving, Lili overheard the landlady say, "They seemed like nice enough people. But can you imagine how stupid this woman must be if she had to write her telephone number on her arm?"

This is a misconception not unfamiliar to other tattooed survivors, and in this circumstance, some might have let it pass. But Lili stormed back inside and delivered a monologue on the subject of those blue numbers. "The worst," says Lili, "was that as Jewish women they should have known better." Lili asked for no apologies, but got one anyway. She also got the apartment.

Another daughter, Bonnie, was born in 1951. To help pay for the house Lili felt they now needed, she took a job as a waitress at the "Famous" Restaurant on Miami Beach, where she worked for twenty-seven years. Her orders were called from the kitchen, as she requested, by number 16—the number of her hut in compound B IIc at Birkenau. Within four years the Zelmonovics had achieved their dream: they were an American family with a house and a secondhand car in the driveway. But the past hovered close, and did not spare the children any more than themselves. Once Bonnie wept at being the only child in her class who could not draw a family tree because, except for her parents and sister, she did not know who her family were.

Lili herself, shopping in downtown Miami one day, suddenly found herself running to "escape" a policeman who had merely been walking in her direction. Thinking that something must be wrong, he ran after her. When he saw how shaken she was, he took her to a Woolworth's lunch counter for a cup of coffee. Very often in the night she would wake up shrieking, the old evils upon her.

In 1958 the popular television show *Queen for a Day* came to Miami for the winter season. The format required the contestants to explain to the host what wish each would want granted if she were crowned Queen for a Day. The winner was selected on the strength of the live-audience applause. Turned down several times to appear on the show, Lili persisted until she was selected to go on the air with four other candidates. When her turn came to explain her wish, Lili said, "Each time I look down at my left arm and see my tattoo, I am reminded of my terrible past in a concentration camp. If only my tattoo could be removed!"

At the end of the show, Lili was crowned Queen for a Day. A few weeks later, when the moment came for the surgical procedure of cutting away the flesh in which the tattoo was embedded, the surgeon routinely prepared to give Lili a local anesthetic.

"No," she said firmly. "I didn't get any anesthetic when they put the tattoo into my arm, and I'm not going to have any anesthetic when it comes out." The number A-10862 was removed without benefit of anesthesia. That was Thanksgiving morning, 1959.

Lili was, in those years, ignorant of the fate of those glass plates back in Prague. They had, in fact, been subject to rather cavalier handling. After thirty photos made from them were published for the first time in Bratislava in 1949 in *The Tragedy of Slovak Jewry,* the plates appear to have been packed away and forgotten in the attic of the Jewish Museum. There they remained for nearly a decade. In 1958 they were accidentally rediscovered by two historians, Ota Kraus and Erich Kulka, who had been rousting about in the attic of the museum when they came upon two boxes marked simply "Auschwitz."

The two men, themselves survivors of the camp and co-authors of an early and important work on the subject called *The Death Factory,* knew instantly the unique value of the glass plates within. In subsequent editions of the book they published a selection of the photos—albeit without attribution. Kulka has, additionally, identified seven SS men and over two dozen surviving prisoners from the photos. Oddly, however, just as Lili did not know of Kraus and Kulka in those years, they did not know of the precise identity or whereabouts of Lili Zelmonovic and her original album.

A number of articles about Lili and her album did finally appear in the press as a result of the interest in Auschwitz generated by the capture in Argentina and the trial in 1961 in Jerusalem of Adolf Eichmann, whose final work for the Reich had been the swift deportation of Hungarian Jewry. Even *Life* magazine sought her out. In 1964 Lili was asked to bring her album to Frankfurt for the trial of twenty-two former SS men who had been posted at Auschwitz-Birkenau.

The prospect of returning to German soil filled Lili with fear, and at first she refused to testify at the trial. The she received an overseas call from one of the prosecutors who, Lili says, asked to speak to her mother. When Lili began to cry the prosecutor apologized, explaining that he had to make her see that she was being asked to testify not for herself, but for those who, like her mother, could not testify for themselves.

During the several nights Lili spent in Frankfurt in December 1964, she was gripped by unreasonable fear. She insisted on having a court-appointed matron sleep on a cot in her hotel room. Even then, she could not close her eyes until she had pushed furniture against the door. At the trial Lili's album provided the only photographic identification of any of the defendants *in situ*—specifically, the SS Blockführer Stefan Baretski on the selection ramp.

This trial also produced a witness who shed first light on the origin of the photos—former SS Hauptscharführer Bernhard Walter, chief of the Identification Service at Auschwitz. He had already served three years in a Polish prison, following his conviction by the war crimes tribunal convened in Cracow in 1947. In preparation for the Frankfurt trial he was interrogated three times between 1958 and 1963 at Fürth, where he worked as a film projectionist.

Under oath, Walter readily admitted that he had been head of the Identification Service. But he insisted that his only job was to take photographs, mug-shot style, of arriving non-Jewish prisoners (Jewish prisoners were not normally photographed). For this purpose, he had a studio and laboratory located in block 17 of the main camp. He was assisted by SS Unterscharführer Ernst Hofmann and a staff of eight prisoners. When Walter was shown copies of photos from the Auschwitz Album, he was vehement in insisting that *he* had not taken them. He had only been to Birkenau once, he claimed, and then only on orders from Berlin to take a panoramic photo of the camp from the main guard tower. While admitting that he had heard talk of the "ramp," he claimed never to have heard the term "selection." Walter did not question the authenticity of the photos. He even admitted that they had an "official character" and obviously had not been taken from "hiding."

Who, then, had taken the photos? Walter could not say for sure. But, in his opinion, it must have been his assistant, Hofmann. Only the two of them were authorized to carry cameras at Auschwitz. For anyone else, it was "strictly forbidden." Walter claimed, moreover, that he never took photos outside the "mother camp." That was the job of Hofmann, the "outside photographer" (*"Aussenfotograf"*).

"It could be," said Walter, "that these photos were made by Hofmann at the order of the Political Service." In the course of the interrogation, Walter's claim that he had never seen the photos turned out to be not quite true. "I can remember having seen photos in the dryer showing groups of Jews," he said. "It is possible that these were from the series of photos taken on the ramp."

Walter came closest to admitting being involved with the Auschwitz Album photos during questioning on February 12, 1962. It did happen, he explained, that "representatives of a very special type of Jewry would be brought to the Identification Service on account of their physical aspect or their dress to be photographed. Perhaps once, two or three persons at a time." This admission may suggest that Walter took the first photo in the album, the only one made under studio conditions.

At the Frankfurt trial Walter appeared as a witness rather than as a defendant. When he repeated his pre-trial testimony that he had never been on the ramp at Birkenau, the defendant Baretski, who is identified in the album, electrified the courtroom by leaping up and shouting at Walter that he was a liar. He, Baretski, had often seen Walter on the ramp—riding his motorcycle, no less.

This outburst was unique in the trial. At no other time did an SS man break ranks to attack another. The court found Baretski's accusation so persuasive that Walter was summarily arrested and held overnight for perjuring himself. Put back on the stand the next day, Walter claimed that he had misunderstood the questions. Yes, it was true that he had been on the ramp—many times. But he continued to insist that he had not taken the photos.

Despite the several interrogations of Walter, the origin and purpose of the Auschwitz Album remain a mystery. According to one theory, it was meant to support the fiction that, as the album title says, the victims were being resettled. But when the Nazis wished to make propaganda, they could do it more persuasively than this—by, for example, staging scenes at rampside canteens and first-aid stations. A propaganda film was, in fact, made during the Hungarian deportations. The first part shows the cruelty of the Hungarian police as they drive young and old into the rail cars from the ghetto at Nagyvarad. The second part is staged to show the "tender" treatment received by the survivors from German nurses when the boxcars are opened at Kassa, where the SS took over from the Hungarian guards.

The inside front cover of the Auschwitz Album is inscribed:

Andenken
von Deinen
Lieben und Unvergesslicher
und Treubleibender
Heinz
("As a remembrance of your dear and unforgettable [*sic*] and faithful Heinz")

Seeing this, the presiding judge at the Frankfurt trial was heard to mutter, "Strange gifts they gave each other." It seems more likely, however, that the inscription dates from a previous use of the album. Written in an unpracticed hand, it contains five errors in six words. The album could have been taken, perhaps, from a prisoner upon arrival at the main camp, emptied of its original contents and refilled with the Birkenau photos. This would have made a unique memento for some SS officer. Even if it did not belong to Walter or Hofmann, the photos surely would have had to be supplied through them.

FOLLOWING her testimony at Frankfurt, Lili went home to Miami and resumed a quiet life of family and work at the "Famous." In the ensuing years, thanks to dissemination of copies made from the glass plates at the Jewish Museum in Prague, certain photos from her album continued to be reproduced in books and periodicals. Copies could also be seen on display at museums around the world. In Jerusalem, for example, at the museum of the official Holocaust Memorial called Yad Vashem, the photos have been enlarged onto panels. Even at the lifeless gray grid of Birkenau, now an official Polish museum, there are strategically placed outdoor billboards featuring immense, grainy reproductions of several photos from the album.

All of these reproductions can be traced back to the glass plates at the Jewish Museum in Prague made from Lili's album in 1946. Despite the ongoing recovery since then of a great and varied body of original documentation of the "final solution," these photos remain the only ones extant which show the arrival of the victims to the greatest of all the killing centers. Yet less than half of the 185 photos in the album had previously been reproduced—and none at all directly from the originals. Given its unique historical stature, it is remarkable that until the summer of 1980 the Auschwitz Album was kept not in an archive or museum but in the bottom drawer of a dresser in the bedroom of a modest home in Miami.

The Auschwitz Album came to the attention of the public in that summer of 1980 through the efforts of Serge and Beate Klarsfeld. This couple, based in Paris, have devoted nearly all the years since their marriage in 1963 to ensuring that neither the victims nor the perpetrators of Nazi crimes be forgotten. Each has proceeded in this work from a different vantage point—he from that of a Jew who lost his father at Auschwitz, she from that of a Berlin-born Protestant whose father served in the Wehrmacht.

The two of them met on a Métro platform in 1960, when he was a graduate student and she an *au pair* girl in the home of a French family. During the ensuing courtship she learned from him about her nation's Nazi past—a subject which had been glossed over in school and at home. From her he came to understand that a new generation of Germans could not be blamed for the crimes of the old. But the honor of their nation could only be regained if that new generation was willing to confront the past and disown it. Beate put that idea foursquare before the world in November 1968 when, at a rally of the Christian Democratic Party in West Berlin, she leaped up on the dais, where Chancellor Kurt Georg Kiesinger was giving a speech, and slapped him full in the face. It was a gesture of disgust that a former executive of Hitler's radio propaganda arm should be leader of the nation. Ten months later Kiesinger lost his bid for re-election. The victor was Willy Brandt, a German who had fought the Nazis until he had to flee his homeland.

In November 1979 the Klarsfelds completed ten years of single-minded effort by forcing the authorities in Cologne to prosecute the three top Nazis active in occupied France. Similar trials had rattled on for years without a clear verdict. This one, however, proceeded in a brisk and organized fashion. The evidence, much of it gathered by the Klarsfelds themselves, was laid out clearly. (Serge, himself a lawyer, represented the 76,000 deportees from France.) In the courtroom each day were young French Jews who took turns traveling to Cologne in order to provide continuity between Jewish life extinguished and renewed.

On February 11, 1980, the three defendants were convicted and sentenced to prison terms which, given their advanced age, were more than symbolic. What was important, however, was not the severity of sentence, but that a new generation of Germans had indeed judged the old. All the jurors had grown up after the war and the presiding judge, who delivered a ringing two-hour judgment, had been a grade-schooler while the Birkenau crematoria were operating at peak capacity.

At the time of the judgment in Cologne, a packet of research materials concerning the vanished Jewish community of Czechoslovakia arrived at the Klarsfeld home in Paris, having been collected in the field by a student named Emmanuel Lulin. In this packet was something unexpected—copies of 70 photos of Jews arriving at Birkenau. About half were familiar to the Klarsfelds, but the rest were a revelation. Lulin reported, moreover, that at the Jewish Museum in Prague there were more than a hundred other photos which had not been sent. All, of course, were from Lili Zelmonovic's album. But the Klarsfelds were still ignorant of that.

Intrigued, the Klarsfelds sent Lulin back to Prague to secure copies of the rest of the photos. While awaiting their arrival, they made a search for all available photos of Jews at Auschwitz which confirmed what they had suspected: except for three "atrocity" photos taken secretly in one of the killing-facility compounds by the Jewish underground and smuggled out to document the genocide occurring there, no other photos were known of Jews at Auschwitz.

The Klarsfelds decided to collect and publish all of these photos, annotated as fully as possible. Along with media-tuned, symbolic acts like the Kiesinger "slap," the couple recognized documentary books as a powerful weapon in their work. In 1978, for example, they had published the "Memorial to the Deportation of the Jews of France," a massive directory of the 76,000 Jews deported from France during the Nazi period. Since many families had been wiped out down to the last infant and grandparent, that volume stood, thirty-five years after the gassings, as their only tombstone.

But the "Memorial" had also been accepted as evidence of murder at the trial in Cologne. In several instances its documentation exposed the defense testimony as a sham. When one defendant claimed, for example, that he had signed a deportation order in the firm belief that the victims were being sent to a labor camp in the East, he was confronted with a page in the "Memorial" showing that twenty-six of the thirty-five potential "workers" were over the age of seventy, and six were octogenarians.

Publication of the Auschwitz photos would be, like the "Memorial," both homage to the victims and a weapon—aimed, in this case, against the neo-Nazis and others who claim that the Holocaust was a hoax. In recent years this proposition has increasingly been advanced. As survivors die out, the proponents of the "hoax" canard could only grow stronger. These photos, however, record the truth. But before they could be properly published, their authenticity had to be established by addressing certain basic questions. Who had taken them? When? Who are the deportees? How had the photos been preserved? Where were the originals now?

Upon Lulin's return from Prague, the Klarsfelds learned the story of Lili's arrival there with her album in 1946. In Cologne they found Rabbi Bernard Farkas, now eighty years old, who remembered well how he had been approached for advice by the young woman in Bodmocli-Deczin. In Frankfurt they examined the summary of Lili's testimony at the Auschwitz trial of 1964 as well as the unpublished but all-important transcripts of the pre-trial interrogations of Bernhard Walter. In Fürth they learned that Walter had died only a year earlier. No trace of his assistant, Hofmann, could be found.

The only key figure who remained to be found was Lili Zelmonovic. Her last known address was the one given to the Frankfurt court in 1964. But directory assistance in Miami had no record of such a party at that address or any other.

Serge Klarsfeld arrived in the United States on July 20, 1980, determined to find out what had happened to Lili and her album. From New York, he hired a private detective who, within thirty-six hours, located Lili at her old address in Miami—only her name was no longer Zelmonovic. Max had died of a heart attack in 1977. Almost two years later she was remarried to Eric Meier, a German-born Jew who, as a refugee during the war, had been a much decorated member of the Free French forces. He had come to America in 1949. It was under his name that the telephone was now listed.

Klarsfeld decided that he would confront Lili directly, without phoning or writing ahead. At two o'clock on a Friday afternoon he arrived at the doorstep of the Meiers' well-kept stucco house on a block of modest houses in a neighborhood which has become almost entirely Cuban. It was a muggy day in Miami. Several rings of the doorbell brought no answer. Then, abruptly, the door opened. An erect, broad-shouldered woman with a strong face and a powerful presence stood in the doorway, blinking in the hard light. At her neck hung, on a fine chain, a Jewish star and, just above it, a pendant that said "Mom." Plainly, she had been awakened from a midday nap. She looked out warily, dark eyes narrowed.

In hesitant, suddenly awkward English, Serge tried to explain that he had come in search of her and the Auschwitz Album. Facts tumbled out about Auschwitz, Prague, Frankfurt, Cologne. But Lili's face did not soften until he blurted out a single piece of information that had been excised twenty years before: "I can tell you your tattoo number from Auschwitz. It is A-10862. And I can also tell you the date on which you got the number. It was July 25, 1944."

There was silence on the doorstep: this was July 25, 1980, the thirty-sixth anniversary of that event.

"Come in," Lili said at last. "I'll give you a cup of coffee and a piece of cake."

Klarsfeld had come hoping to convince Lili to donate her album to a suitable institution, his own choice being Yad Vashem in Jerusalem. If she did not want to do that, he was carrying $10,000 cash in his briefcase with which he hoped to buy the album and turn it over himself to Yad Vashem. But this precaution was unnecessary. Lili and Eric had already decided, earlier that year, that they would donate the album to the "right place." They simply were not yet sure of how to proceed. Now, with the arrival of this stranger, Lili was convinced that Providence had intervened, just as she knew that it must when she had found the album as a teen-ager. It was indeed time to give up the album, and the "right place" for it was Yad Vashem. Lili discussed this not only with Eric but with her daughters, Esther and Bonnie, for she had promised the album to them and to their children, Scot Martin, Gary Michael and Michael.

Lili donated the Auschwitz Album on August 27, 1980, in the largest such ceremony ever held at Yad Vashem.* As she handed it over to Yitzhak Arad, director of the institution, she kissed the ragged album as if it were a holy book. In one of the speeches that followed this moment, Minister of Education Zevulun Hammer said that it was fitting that such a document, which represented the nadir of the Jewish people, should come to rest in Jerusalem, which represented that people reborn.

*In the previous week, the nonprofit Beate Klarsfeld Foundation had published 1,000 copies of a scholarly edition of the album. As with the foundation's many other publications documenting the Holocaust, it was distributed free to libraries, archives and research centers around the world.

Epilogue

From Jerusalem, Lili went with Eric to Birkenau. "I had to do it," she explains, "because what happened to me there has always seemed unreal. I could never really believe that my family had gone up in smoke there, that it was not a dream. By going back, I felt that maybe finally I would believe it. Then I could say good-bye, and a stone would come off my heart."

Lili and Eric arrived in Cracow on the evening of August 29, 1980, and went the next morning by taxi to the busy but charmless small city of Oświeçim. The narrow road that leads from the main camp to Birkenau does not seem to have been paved since Nazi times. The countryside is low, bleak and lonely, as it was when the deportation trains approached on the adjacent rail spur. The main guard tower looms first on the uninterrupted horizon, then the barbed wire cordon, then the grid of low huts. Even from afar, a malevolent spirit seems to reach out from the place.

A quarter of a mile away, Lili asked the taxi driver to stop so that she could walk the rest of the way. Beside her was Eric, who wore for this visit the red beret issued to him by the Free French paratroopers. As they set out, it began to drizzle. In the field to their right, three peasants were hand-scything grain and tossing it into a slant-sided, horse-drawn wagon. Lili had once pulled a similar wagon through these fields. On the left side of the road, parked near the camp entrance, was a red, purple and gold tour bus from France, fully loaded and gleamingly chic under the lowering sky. The passengers looked out dubiously, as if they had little inclination to leave their luxurious interior for the drizzle, mud and evil of the camp.

From their windows, these passengers could now see a curious sight. Coming up the road toward the arch of the guard tower, huddled beside a man in a red beret, was a handsome middle-aged woman who, despite the emptiness all around, was hunched up as if at any moment she expected to be clubbed down. The act of walking seemed to be taking all her strength, concentration and courage. It was as if she were walking into a strong wind, but there was none. The watchers could not know that this walk was as hard as anything she ever had to do—that it was a willful re-entry into the domain where nightmare had begun.

Then she was through the door beside the archway of the guard tower where the trains had entered, and it was easier. The great network of compounds within compounds, fences enclosing fences, was lifeless. Some huts had long ago been burned, leaving only their chimneys. Others stood as before, their rough wood walls blackened with age. Lili approached a hut and swung open a creaky door. It was dank inside, and a stripe of gray light from the clerestory windows fell on the warren of triple-tiered sleeping pallets. A normal-sized person, crawling to the center level of a tier on which five people lay, could barely lift the head or knees. From the position farthest in, it was impossible to see out. It made one feel like a bug or a rodent.

All that is left of the killing facilities at the western end of the ramp are piles of debris—very substantial piles. The underground gas chambers, long and deep, are filled with shards and wedges of concrete from the dynamited roof through which SS men once knelt to drop poison and from which the screams and rattles from so many throats arose. Swamp water has seeped up in the crevices to form pools where water spiders dart. Just as the tiers of pallets in the huts are more constricting than the photos would suggest, the gas chambers are more commodious.

Lili's first task of her trip, less than a week earlier, had been to deliver the Auschwitz Album to Yad Vashem. Standing at this spot, she undertook her second task. She prayed at the graveside for the souls of her parents. This she did calmly and in silence. Then she turned, unmindful of the mud, and with her usual strong stride and proud carriage renewed, left this place forever.

Note

    The original photos in the Auschwitz Album, as it was presented to Yad Vashem, are published here. Five additional photos, made from the glass-plate negatives of 1946, are included by courtesy of the Jewish Museum in Prague. These copies replace photos that Lili Meier later gave away to survivors or, in two cases, to courts in order that SS men might be identified on the Birkenau ramp. A small number, not more than six, of the original photos are still missing.

    Tucked into the back of the album when Lili found it was a set of ten pages displaying sixty-three small photos of subjects that include the physical plant at Auschwitz and official visits to the camp. These are reproductions rather than original photos. They have been omitted here, as have two photos of the crematorium at Dora which were taped onto the last of the fifty-six pages of the album.

    Except for the five Prague pictures, all the photos published here were made individually from the originals at Yad Vashem. The actual size of each of the photos is 3¼″ x 4⅜″.

Resettlement of Jews from Hungary

Umsiedlung der Juden aus Ungarn

When Lili Jacob first opened this album in 1945, she immediately recognized, in the photo at right, the chief rabbi of her own community. Naftali Svi Weiss came from a line of Hasidic rabbis founded by his grandfather Josef Weiss in the Transylvanian town of Spinka. His father, Rabbi Isaac Weiss, was said to be a man with a gaze so piercing that one glance was enough to send schoolboys at play dashing off to study.

Rabbi Weiss had come to Bilke in 1929 at the age of thirty-nine. When he arrived, he was received like a sovereign: a specially decorated, horse-drawn coach took him from the station to the synagogue. His congregants lined the road, cheering and waving banners of welcome.

Rabbi Weiss established in Bilke a "Spinka" yeshiva, which soon attracted students from afar. On Thursday nights the rabbi would personally conduct gas-lit oral examinations of the students, in two shifts of about thirty each. It was often after midnight before he was satisfied with the results. On other nights, excepting the Sabbath, the rabbi studied alone until very late. A disciple remembers coming into his study one night and finding the rabbi engrossed in a text, his feet in a pail of ice water to keep himself awake.

As the Nazi shadow spread over Europe, an American congregation wrote to invite Rabbi Weiss to become their spiritual leader. He answered that he would not forsake his own congregation. When the train carrying the Jews of Bilke was about to reach its destination, one of the fearful people asked, "Rabbi, what will happen to us?"

At that moment the train curved off the main line onto the Birkenau spur. "Listen to the sound of the wheels screaming" was the rabbi's only answer.

2

This photograph, unique in the album, was made in a studio environment. The only facility for this work at Auschwitz-Birkenau was the SS Identification Service located in block 17 of the main camp. Here photographs, mug-shot style, were made of all arriving prisoners except gypsies and Jews, who were not normally photographed. But Bernard Walter, director of the Identification Service, testified in 1962 that "Jews of a special type" had been sent to the studio—"for example, rabbis in their traditional costume." Walter did not say who ordered these photos or for what purpose or if it happened more than once. But the Nazis took an interest in preserving a record of the race they intended to extinguish, including even skeletons that were sent from Birkenau back to the Reich. Adolf Eichmann himself, at his first meeting with Jewish leaders in Budapest on March 31, 1944, claimed that he was "personally very interested in Jewish historical artifacts and literature," and asked to be assigned a guide for a tour of the local Jewish museum.

2

3

Arrival
of a Transport

Ankunft eines Transportzuges

The Birkenau arrival platform, known simply as the "ramp," was completed only weeks before this photo was taken. For the first time, Jews could be delivered right up under the shadow of the crematoria chimneys. Formerly, they had to be transferred from train to trucks at another platform half a mile outside the gates of Birkenau.

Here, members of the SS "ramp" team take their stations in front of each boxcar of the newly arrived train on the right. On command, they will unbolt all the doors. Due to the unprecedented crush of transports destined for the ramp in this late spring of 1944—the peak period of the Hungarian deportations—two trains were often alongside simultaneously, with others backed up and waiting for a day or longer.

Debris litters the ground in front of the hastily emptied train on the left, which is about to be sent back for a new deportation. Judging by the sharp shadows in the rising sun, the time would be early in the morning.

5

This train brings about 3,000 Carpathian Jews, including a group from Bilke. They had been en route for two and a half days with little food or water and no sanitary facilities other than a bucket. Here they have been tumbled out of the boxcars, cramped, dazed, hungry and parched but, for the most part, under their own power thanks to a comparatively short trip and clement weather. Some trains were in transit for many days and arrived in the heat of summer or the dead of winter; few who traveled on them were capable of obeying the order to disembark. When the Jewish community of Corfu arrived after twenty-seven days in transit by boat and train, the doors were opened to total stillness.

10

Hungary was in the vanguard of European nations to enact anti-Jewish laws. However, during the first four years of the war it stopped short at the ultimate measure of deportation —except for the expulsion in 1941 of 18,000 Jews who could not prove Hungarian citizenship. With the German occupation on March 19, 1944, Hungary relented. The pretext for the deportations was that the Germans were demanding 10,000 Jewish slave laborers for their arms industry. When asked why, in addition to the able-bodied, they were deporting the very young, old and infirm, the rationale offered was that the workers would be more productive if their families were nearby. Here on the ramp, the families still believed in the fiction of the "family camp."

Another attempt was made to throw a shroud of legitimacy over the deportations from Sub-Carpathian Ruthenia and northern Transylvania by declaring the region to be a "Military Operational Zone" from which the "Judeo-Bolsheviks" would have to be evacuated as the Red Army approached from the East. The decree was issued on April 12, 1944, three days before the Jews were forced into ghettos.

12

Mayoral responsibility

The persons to be transported are to be supplied with bread for two days. The two days' supply per person is 400 grams. Taking along of additional food is prohibited... The Mayor will also see to it that each car is provided with a covered bucket (for sanitary purposes) and with a can suitable for drinking water. It is the responsibility of the Mayor to supply 90 locks with keys per transport... It should be remembered that the transports will also include German cars which cannot be locked unless a 30-centimeter chain is first used, which will then be locked... If necessary, as many as 100 may be put in a car. They can be loaded like sardines, since the Germans require hardy people. Those who cannot take it will perish. There is no need in Germany for ladies of fashion.

> —Confidential orders to mayors of cities in Carpathian-Ruthenia and northern Transylvania containing ghettos (drawn up one week before the deportations commenced, at a meeting in Mukachevo between the Hungarian police and the Gestapo). Full text in Randolph Braham's The Politics of Genocide.

The stripe-suited prisoners are members of the unit called "Canada," assigned to clear the boxcars of luggage and debris. This was a much-sought-after assignment, since it held the prospect of being able to filch food out of the abandoned parcels. The prisoners were searched, however, after each shift. If found with any booty, they would be punished by severe beating or even death. They had to surreptitiously swallow whatever they found—a crust of bread, a bit of salami, a fig—as they worked.

14

The woman conversing with the slave in the foreground of the picture on the right is probably seeking information about this place and her fate. Though he knew full well what her fate would be, he or any member of "Canada" was forbidden to reveal it. Those who asked about the flames and smoke often seen belching from the chimneys in the background were told that this was a bakery or factory. An incident is recounted by a surviving "Canadian" of a colleague who told a newly arrived woman point-blank that she and her son would shortly go up in smoke. She confronted an SS officer, demanding to know the truth. He assuaged her fears. The slave was allowed to finish the work shift and then, for his indiscretion, was beaten to death.

Under the direction of the SS, columns are quickly formed—men on one side, women and children on the other. The people have been told that the larger pieces of luggage they have left behind will be delivered directly to their new quarters. Those who wish, and who have the strength, are allowed to carry smaller bundles, briefcases, waterbuckets, blankets and baskets.

Elsewhere in the camp, savagery reigned, as these people would shortly discover. But here on the ramp, the SS endeavored to be "correct," limiting their use of force to an occasional prodding with the cane. This was a departure from previous practice when clubs, attack dogs and summary shootings were the norm. The new policy, as exercised here, arose from pragmatic rather than humane considerations. The calmer such a large body of people could be kept, the easier the job of the SS would be.

The woman in the center of photo 19, smiling and with her arm raised, appears to recognize someone in the crowd.

20

For a few moments, as the boxcars continue to empty, there is disorganization on the ramp. At last, people can stretch and breathe fresh air. They look around apprehensively, wondering where they are. During the trip the tallest among them had peered out of the small, high windows, trying to guess where they were being taken. Moshe Avital, who arrived on one of these transports, remembers that when someone caught sight of the "KL" (Konzentrationslager) sign just outside the Birkenau gates, he took the "L" to mean they must be approaching Lublin. That's where it had been rumored the Jews were to be resettled. Few if any of the arrivees had ever heard of Auschwitz.

Selection

Arriving trains at Birkenau were pushed by a yard locomotive through the archway of the main guard tower (far left of photo) to the selection platform. Given the hectic pace of the Hungarian transports, the archway entrance could be a busy place. An ironic incident from this period—one which gave rare but immense satisfaction to the inmates—is recorded by a survivor named Judith Steinberg Newman:

One evening a locomotive which had just delivered a fresh transport of Hungarian Jews was backing swiftly out of the main gate. At the same moment, a car carrying officers of the SS selection team was speeding to the platform. There was a "terrible collision," reports Mrs. Newman, who had herself just been marched out of the camp as part of a labor brigade headed for the night shift at a munitions factory. Looking back, dumfounded, the women saw the SS car lying squashed beneath the nose of the locomotive. Two of the SS had been killed and three others injured.

"We took a deep breath," writes Mrs. Newman, "and felt for the first time that there was justice in the world, after all."

Here the photographer apparently has climbed on top of a box-car toward the front of the train and is looking down directly on the infamous selection point. Until this moment, whatever the arriving families had suffered, they had at least suffered together. But now, at the whim of the selection team headed by the now infamous Dr. Josef Mengele, these families would be splintered forever.

The head of the long column on the far side of the tracks in photo 26 has nearly reached killing facility No. 1, visible at the top of the picture. On the second floor of this facility, above the crematoria ovens, lived a prisoner-doctor named Miklos Nyiszli. Upon his arrival in May of 1944, he had been chosen by Dr. Mengele to be camp pathologist. From his room, Dr. Nyiszli commanded a "direct view of the tracks."

On his first morning in residence, Dr. Nyiszli was awakened early by the whistle of an arriving transport. From his window, he watched. The selection took, he estimates, "scarcely half an hour." Then the left-hand column, like the one in this photo, started its walk to the killing center. This took "five to six minutes." By the time the people went through the gate into the courtyard, they were right under his window.

"The children's eyes were heavy with sleep," he reports, "and they clung to their mothers' clothes." In the courtyard, the SS allowed the people to fill their cups and bottles from the lawn spigots and then waited patiently while they slaked their thirst. Within the building, meanwhile, Dr. Nyiszli could hear the whirring of the fifteen high-speed ventilators which were already fanning the crematoria fires.

27

Of his moment facing the SS selector, the psychoanalyst Viktor Frankl writes in **Man's Search for Meaning**: *"He was a tall man who looked slim and fit in his spotless uniform. What a contrast to us, who were untidy and grimy after our long journey! He had assumed an attitude of careless ease, supporting his right elbow with his left hand. His right hand was lifted, and with the forefinger of that hand he pointed very leisurely to the right or left. . . .*

"It was my turn. . . . The SS man looked me over, appeared to hesitate, then put both his hands on my shoulders. I tried very hard to look smart, and he turned my shoulders very slowly until I faced right, and I moved over to that side." Only that night did Frankl learn, from a veteran prisoner, the fate of those who were sent left—about 90 percent of his convoy. This was done not by words, but with a gesture to the heavens.

The elegant woman in the foreground stares beyond the camera to where, most probably, other members of her family have already been sent following selection. Note the intensity with which the man just behind her, hat in hand, also peers at somebody unseen. The column behind him, on the other side of the tracks, is marching toward killing facility No. 2.

This was the last moment to catch a glimpse of a loved one. Viktor Frankl writes of how, in the long days of ensuing slavery, his mind's eye "clung to my wife's image, imagining it with uncanny acuteness. I heard her answering me, saw her smile, her frank and encouraging look. . . . Had I known that my wife was dead, I think I would have still given myself, undisturbed by that knowledge, to the contemplation of her image, and that my mental conversation with her would have been just as vivid and just as satisfying."

These two young women are being sent to the right for processing as slaves. Had they been mothers, they would have been sent with their children to death.

When Lili Jacob (then a contemporary of these young women) was sent to the right, she impulsively dashed back to join her mother and her youngest brothers, who had been ordered to go to the left. For this act she was stabbed in the arm by an SS guard. Though Lili had her tattooed serial number removed from her arm long ago, the angry scar from that incident remains.

With a poke of his cane, the SS man in the center of the photo directs the old woman in black, who holds the hand of an infant, to join the others who are crematorium-bound across the tracks.

The truck at right has already been loaded with baggage by the "Canada" brigade. It is headed toward the warehouse compound, where the contents will be sorted and recycled. Bicycles, like the one alongside the truck, became a common mode of transportation for SS men as times grew more difficult for the German war machine. The finely tailored uniform worn by the prisoner at lower left was probably made for him, through barter, by other prisoners skilled in the needle trades. Making a good appearance was more than vanity; it signified to other prisoners and the SS alike that this man had "connections," and merited respect. At the other extreme were the "Muslims" —prisoners who had lost all hope and whom the SS men often killed as idly as if they were flies.

The man at right has been identified as the SS man Stefan Baretski. He killed many prisoners and was particularly feared for his ability to take a life with a single chop of his hand to an artery. At the trial of twenty-two SS men that took place in Frankfurt in 1963–65, Simon Gotland, a Polish-born member of the "Canada" ramp team, told the court of an incident concerning Baretski that throws light on the courageous humanity of a prisoner as well as on the inhumanity of his keeper. A train had arrived on which "all were sick." Baretski gave the ramp team twenty minutes to empty the cars. Entering one, Gotland found a woman who had just given birth. He wrapped the infant in a cloth and placed it next to her. Against strict standing orders, he got a food package from another car and brought it to her.

Then Baretski came. "Why are you playing around with this filth?" he yelled at Gotland. Then he kicked the baby away "like a football."

Taken aback, Judge Hofmeyer asked, "Can you swear to that in good conscience?"

"I can swear with a pure heart," Gotland answered, "that it was a hundred percent worse than I have described it." Then, showing his decency now as he had shown it on the ramp, the witness added, "I am not an evil man. Perhaps they were sick when they did it. My wounds had already healed, but now they are bleeding again."

The gate at the upper left corner of the photo leads to the section of the camp on the south side of the ramp known as B I. Begun in the winter of 1941–42, it was the first section of Birkenau to be built. Its first inmates were men, among them Russian POWs. By the late summer of 1943, it was used only for women, whose numbers were permitted to grow with the need for slave labor. Women in B I and, across the buffer zone, men in B II would steal up to their respective electrified fences whenever they could, hoping to catch sight of loved ones on the other side. Months or years could pass without their knowing whether, a bare few hundred yards away, a member of their family had survived.

33

Several old-fashioned prams can be seen abandoned in front of the pole at the center of the photo on the right. The infants are almost certainly in the arms of family members in the far column heading for killing facility No. 2. No records—least of all of the infants—have been preserved, of these deportees who went directly to their deaths. Consequently, their numbers will never be precisely known. But in 1946, before the International Military Tribunal at Nuremberg, a survivor named S. Szmaglewska was asked how many prams were sent at the end of each day to the storeroom where she worked. "Sometimes there were a hundred," the witness answered, "sometimes even a thousand."

35

Survivors of the selection often remark on the large number of SS men swarming over the ramp. Twelve are visible in this photo alone.

36

In photo 37, the man standing between the columns is missing his pants and one shoe. It is not unlikely that during the voyage here he became unhinged. This was a common occurrence in the crowded and darkened boxcars, where the deportees were beset by thirst, dirtied by excreta and confronted by corpses.

The woman just selected to go to the left in this photo might well have been ordered to the right if she did not carry an infant. In the tradition of an Orthodox wife, her hair is covered. When young Fannie Schwimmer of Bilke stood in this line holding the infant child of her sister Leah, she was approached by a "Canada" member who knew by her "beautiful" black hair that she was unmarried. He whispered to her to give the child back to its mother. Unaware of the consequences, Fannie did so. She was sent to the right, while Leah, with the infant now in her arms, was sent to the left.

Men
on Arrival

Männer bei der Ankunft

39

40

41

The men in the photo above are dressed in the style of Orthodox Jews of Sub-Carpathian Ruthenia. They wore their square-crowned black dress hats only with their best clothing on the Sabbath—or on the occasion of a trip away from home. They are all too old to be selected for work. The boy at the far left is too young.

The old man at the center of photo 42 keeps his place with the able-bodied even though he is peglegged and must support himself with a crutch and cane.

The man and boy at left appear to be father and son. As with mothers and daughters, the desire to keep a parent alive often impelled a young man to survive. "I had my father," Ben Edelbaum writes of his first days as a fifteen-year-old at Birkenau after four years in the Lodz ghetto. "I was in proud possession of the only human being with whom I could manage to retain a direct link with my prewar past, and who constantly assured me that my memories were all real and not a dream . . . I knew one thing for sure: I was going to hold on to him with all my might, with all my heart, with all my mind, using every conceivable method or deceit available at my very limited disposal."

They did survive Birkenau together, but at another work camp the father died of disease. Even then, the "slightly raised ground" of the mass grave outside the camp fence where his father had been dumped became the focus of Edelbaum's will to live. Each day, he writes, "I'd turn my eyes in the direction of the grave and pray to God to let me survive these horrors in order to carry on the worthy name of my father."

The boy shown here is a few years younger than Edelbaum had been upon arrival. The usual cut-off age for work was anywhere from twelve to fifteen, depending on the need for slaves, the whim of the selector, luck—and sometimes on fast thinking. When Edelbaum and his father were waiting in line, they observed that the selector was alternating in sending people to the left and right. Neither father nor son knew which was "better." But they got somebody else in the line to go between them so that they might go in the same direction.

48

49

50

Doctors were often put in a group of their own on the ramp, to make it easier for SS doctors to interview them. While only the two men in the center wear Red Cross armbands, it is possible that others in this distinguished-looking group are also doctors.

In the picture on the right, the grim-faced man wearing the dark hat in the center can be recognized, shorn and in a striped uniform, at the front left of photo 128 and at left in photo 129.

This photo calls to mind an eyewitness account of the beating and gassing of nearly 2,000 young boys at killing facility No. 2 in October 1944, a harrowing event even by Birkenau standards. It was recorded in the journal of a prisoner named Salmen Lewental. He did not survive, but his journal (included in "Amidst a Nightmare of Crime," published by the State Museum of Auschwitz) was one of several found buried in bottles and canisters on the grounds of the crematoria after the war. "The boys looked so handsome and were so well-built that even [their] rags did not mar their beauty," he writes. Then, in harrowing detail, he recounts how, stripped naked and wailing, they were chased around the crematorium compound by club-wielding SS men until all had at last been pushed into the gas chamber. Of these SS he writes: "Their joy was indescribable." Lewental ends the account and, indeed, the entire journal by asking: "Didn't they ever have children of their own?"

53

54

It was thirst rather than hunger that proved most unbearable during the trip to Birkenau, especially as summer approached. In many of the photographs, as in the one on the right, the deportees are carrying cups, flasks or bottles. An important tool the Germans used to ensure obedience without overt violence was to keep the people thirsty. They were led to believe that the faster and more smoothly the selection went, the sooner they could fill their water vessels and drink.

Women
on Arrival

Frauen bei der Ankunft

57

58

Note how killing facility No. 2, with its great bulk and tall chimney, can be seen over the boxcars behind the group of women and children in photo 59.

The minimum age to qualify for work was about fifteen, but for a younger, strong-looking child, the rule could be stretched. The SS selectors did not bother to check birth dates. On the opposite page, the girl at the right, grouped with the older women and younger children, had not made the grade. Her mother has probably been selected for work and she has been told to escort her younger siblings to the "family camp." When people asked when they would again see the members of their family selected for work, the reassuring answer was: "Visiting day is on Sunday."

63

64

65

66

After the Selection, Still-Able-bodied Men

Nach der Aussortierung noch einsatzfähige Männer

As the war progressed, all Jewish men in Hungary between the ages of eighteen and forty-eight were subject to service in labor brigades attached to the army. These brigades did all manner of heavy labor both at and behind the front. Under Nazi influence, the treatment the men received grew steadily worse. On the Ukrainian front they suffered terribly. A notorious incident occurred on April 30, 1943, at Doroshich, where 800 Jewish servicemen suffering from typhus had been quartered in a barn. The Hungarians set fire to the barn, and when those inside tried to escape, they were machine-gunned by their own "comrades."

The Germans were incensed at any instance of humane treatment of the labor servicemen. Discovering in early June 1944 that a unit of 400 men had been given a ten-day furlough, they intercepted the train on which the men were returning to duty and rerouted it to Birkenau. This action was carried out by Hungarian police.

Since most of the men in the photos on the facing page wear the Star of David rather than the armband, it is unlikely that they were then members of a labor brigade, but they do give the appearance of having recently been in a military unit. Some wear military-style gaiters, for example, and the man in the center foreground of photo 66 carries his blanket over the right shoulder as a soldier would. The man in photo 49 actually wears, along with an armband, the hat officially issued to Jewish labor servicemen.

67

The column of men in the photo at left has been selected for work and is being marched from the ramp into the vast section of the camp called B II. Behind them are great piles of property belonging to the deportees. The fence is electrified and at night, when the guard was withdrawn, the power was turned on.

68

The head of a young boy can be seen amid the men at the right of the photo. Normally, such a child would have been sent to die with his mother, but sometimes a boy would be taken as a "pipl," or personal page, to one of the guards. Some children were chosen for pseudomedical experiments and a few were put in labor brigades of their own. Jehuda Bacon, for example, was twelve when he arrived at Birkenau. He ended up as a member of a team of twenty children who pulled a cart. "We got ashes from Crematorium II and scattered them on icy roads," he says. "When there were no people in the gas chambers, the Kapo [trustee] let us warm ourselves there."

The men in these photos are, according to the album's German caption, fit for work (einsatzfähige). It is not clear, then, why the much older and weaker-appearing men at the right of this photo have been included among them. In any case, the Lagerstrasse, onto which they have just come from the ramp, led both to the actual disinfection center known as the "sauna" as well as to the three killing facilities that were located at the west end of B II. Therefore, both those destined to live and die passed along this route. Here, however, all the men appear to be merely standing in ranks rather than moving along. Backups on the Lagerstrasse were common during the period of the Hungarian deportations. Often one transport of 3,500 people had yet to be processed before the next arrived. And so the people waited on the Lagerstrasse until their turn came.

Still-Able-bodied Women

Noch einsatzfähige Frauen

These women have been selected for work. They have been sent from the ramp across the tracks to stand at the side of the main road through the camp. As they wait the women stand with their backs to the crematoria. They may have been placed this way so that they would not see what happens to other columns marching in that direction.

The two women in the foreground of photo 82, bearing a strong resemblance to each other, could well be mother and daughter. While it was normal SS practice on the ramp to send young mothers with small children directly to their death, it was not unusual, by 1944, for an older woman to be picked for work along with her grown daughter—provided that she appeared vigorous.

Older women would not be expected to last long at hard physical labor, but they could be useful at one of the many factories operating around Auschwitz. At this late date in the war, the ramp was also a major supplier of slaves to work camps and factories elsewhere in the domain of the Reich.

A number of Birkenau daughters, selected with their mothers for work, have said that it was their determination to keep their mothers alive that became their own prime motive for survival. "Mother" was, in those circumstances, a relative term. When thirteen-year-old Halina Birenbaum's mother was gassed, the child's sister-in-law Hela said, "I will be your mother now." Though the two had not previously been close, Hela was true to her word until she grew too weak to care for Halina. Then the roles were reversed. When Hela was selected from a parade of naked women for gassing while the tiny but still strong Halina was selected for life, the child desperately implored the women's camp commandant Hössler to rescind the selection. Amused at this presumption, Hössler agreed. This extraordinary victory, however, merely postponed the inevitable. At the end, the shriveled Hela looked up at Halina from her sleeping pallet with the big, all-trusting eyes of an infant.

83

84

Like those headed for the killing facilities, these women selected for work have been permitted to carry small suitcases, bundles, cups and small pots. Once they arrive at the door of the sauna for disinfection, they will have to give up these items along with their clothing. Behind the women, the slaves of the "Canada" brigade can be seen toiling amid the great piles of belongings left behind. The ramp must be clean before the arrival of the next transport.

Women entering the camp from the ramp, like these, regularly saw beside the fences emaciated and filthy prisoners who lethargically sat and picked at lice. Once such a state of apathy was reached, few survived. And so, that condition had to be fought. "My first impulse," writes Reska Weiss in **Journey Through Hell,** *"was to concentrate on making myself more presentable. Under the circumstances this may sound ludicrous; what real relation was there between my new-found spiritual resistance and the unsightly rags on my body? But in a subtle sense there* was *a relationship....I began to look around me and saw the beginning of the end for any woman who had the opportunity to wash and had not done so, or any woman who felt that the tying of a shoe-lace was wasted energy."*

86

87

88

These women are probably headed for processing at the sauna. The men in the background are in block B IId, where 20,000 generally able-bodied men were imprisoned. They were not forbidden to stare at the women, as they do here, but conversation could be struck up only at the risk of severe punishment.

The windowless, prefabricated hut in which these men lived was standard at Birkenau. It had originally been designed as a stable for fifty-two horses. Here it served as shelter for as many as a thousand prisoners. The only available light filtered through a narrow line of clerestory windows along the upper roof line. On the right side of the entrance doors was a single room belonging to the Blockältester *(senior block prisoner). Then came a warren of triple-decker pallets onto which the prisoners were crammed. The few mattresses that were sometimes available were filled with wood shavings. A stove with a single heating pipe ran down the center of the hut. There was no toilet, but a bucket was placed at the rear of the hut for night-time use.*

No Longer Able-bodied Men

Nicht mehr einsatzfähige Männer

These old people were among those who, unable to stand during selection on the ramp, were allowed to remain where they had disembarked. Some who could have walked elected to stay with those who could not.

In time these people would be put on a truck, to be delivered to one of the killing facilities. Once at the destination, the driver would activate the mechanism that lifted the back of the van, dump-truck style, until all those inside had slid out onto the ground in a heap.

91

92

82

93

Orthodox Jews wear beards according to biblical law. A convenient way for Nazi thugs to torment such Jews was to pull at the beard, slash at it, forcibly shave it, or even rip it out of the flesh. In the ghettos, men were frequently ordered by the authorities to shave off their beards as well as hair, ostensibly as a hygienic measure. While vermin that could infest hair was a problem where people were incarcerated without bathing facilities, the shaving of beards was just as surely another form of degradation. That was the case in the ghetto of Berehovo, where the Jewish community of Bilke was held prior to deportation to Birkenau. Only a few of the elders, like Rabbi Weiss, were allowed to keep their beards.

Two men in these photos—one old and one quite young—wear scarfs around their faces to hide their shame.

103

104

The photographer has here assembled several Hasidic Jews for a series of group portraits. The corner of the hat of Rabbi Weiss of Bilke can be seen in the lower left-hand corner of photo 105. (The photo on the first page of the album shows him fully.) The others in the photos are not from Bilke.

Orthodox Jewish men like those in photo 103 would never remove their hats unless forced to do so.

The photos of this group appear to have been taken at the west end of the main camp road, almost directly in front of the fence enclosing killing facility No. 1.

106

107

The three men in photo 108 look like leaders of their community. Even after days in the boxcars, they manage to be only a little rumpled. They are, nevertheless, too old to have been spared for work and it seems likely that they are on their way to die along with the Orthodox men and children behind them on the Lagerstrasse.

91

This photo is the only one in the album in which as many SS men are visible as Jews (four of each). It is the only one in which the anxieties of a deportee have erupted into physical struggle. And it is the only known photo which shows clearly, in the background, the long, low killing facility No. 3 during the time when it was "on line." Like its twin, No. 4, it was hidden in the forest, quite invisible from the ramp. The path on which this woman apparently refuses to travel leads to the door of the dressing room. The portion of the building to the left contains the gas chambers. Out of sight to the right is the portion containing the ovens.

The SS was constantly on the alert for trouble here on the doorstep of the killing centers. It was here that, despite all blandishments, the people sometimes ceased to believe that they would really get the shower they longed for. In his memoirs, camp commandant Rudolf Höss writes that "difficult individuals were picked out early on and most carefully supervised. At the first signs of unrest, those responsible were unobtrusively led behind the building and killed with a small-calibre gun that was inaudible to the others."

Once the order was given to undress, the situation frequently went out of control. Höss writes that "women would suddenly give the most terrible shrieks while undressing, or tear their hair or scream like maniacs…and would call down every imaginable curse upon our heads." Threats no longer worked. It was only when the women were told they were upsetting their children that they would go to their death calmly. On one occasion a woman from a French transport managed to grab a pistol away from an SS man and shoot him dead.

In this facility, on October 7, 1944, the Sonderkommando *itself revolted. The members killed several SS men and blew up the crematorium with dynamite smuggled to them by Birkenau women who worked in an ammunition factory. A large SS force put down the revolt and caught those prisoners who had escaped. Nearly all who were involved were shot. The women who had procured the explosives, led by twenty-four-year-old Roza Robata, were tortured before they were executed.*

110

These old and crippled people are unable to make the walk toward the killing centers along the Lagerstrasse, visible to the right of the base of the guard tower. Like the pile of pots, jugs and crates piled behind them in photo 111, they wait for removal.

Except for the selection panorama, where it could hardly be avoided, the photographer has taken pains to keep SS men out of these photos. Here, however, the elongated shadow of an SS man with his cane darkens the foreground.

No Longer Able-bodied Women and Children

Nicht mehr einsatzfähige Frauen u. Kinder

Though the mother of these children is no longer with them, it is perhaps the grandmother who has carefully tucked their scarfs inside their coats.

This is the only photo in the Auschwitz Album in which no faces can be seen. Yet there is none which is more poignant.

Behind this old woman an invalid can be seen in a bentwood convalescent rocker. Many pieces of furniture arrived at Birkenau in this way. The scene in this photo is just to the left of that in photo 90.

113

98

114

115

The narrow-gauge rails on which the children stand, here on the Lagerstrasse, were part of a system on which supply carts were pushed by hand throughout the camp.

118

The barracks in the background are part of block B IIc, known as the Hungarian women's camp. Like the men's block B IId on the opposite side of the Lagerstrasse, it was originally designed as stables; it consisted of 34 huts, in which 30,000 prisoners lived.

Note that the woman at far left of photo 118 appears to be in an advanced state of pregnancy. Sometimes, when the doors of the gas chambers were opened following a gassing, women were found to have given birth in the act of dying.

These women and children are walking on the Lagerstrasse. After nearly a half-mile walk they will turn left toward the killing facility just beyond, to the more primitive gassing station, Bunker 5. Those who have been selected for work will also walk this way. But they will continue on a short distance past the killing-facility gates to the sauna for processing.

120

121

122

123

The building in the background might be mistaken for an administrative center or a dining hall, but behind the double windows are fifteen high-speed ovens, vented through the massive central chimney. Extending underground from the west end of the building (killing facility No. 2), are the dressing room and the gas chamber. Automatic elevators brought the fresh corpses up to the crematory level. Also on this level was a smelter room, where the extracted dental gold and silver were processed into ingots. There was a room on the second floor where, utilizing heat rising from below, women's hair was hung on lines after washing to dry for future use. Behind the small dormer windows were the quarters of the Sonderkommando, which was kept isolated from the rest of the camp.

The huts just visible in the background at right are in the men's hospital compound. The west side of these huts looked out both on this facility and, further to the rear, to killing facility No. 3. Wieslaw Kielar, a Polish orderly assigned to the hospital compound, reports that by standing on a cot and looking out the gable window of one of the huts, he was able to look over a "concealing hedge" and observe "Dantesque scenes." Despite having seen a "great deal" during his previous three years at the camp, what he saw there was "still such a shock... that one lost one's belief in everything, even in God."

*Remarkably, some members of the **Sonderkommando** itself managed to keep their faith. Camp pathologist Miklos Nyiszli writes of a deeply religious member of the unit who insisted on whispering a prayer over each of the dead that he handled—an unceasing occupation. Nyiszli intervened with the SS on behalf of this "ascetic," arranging for him to be shifted to the job of burning piles of debris deemed unworthy of recycling (e.g., rags, bags, prayer books, family photos) that were always piling up in front of killing facility No. 2. Such a pile can be seen in this photo.*

Except for photographs made during construction, this is the only known picture clearly showing either of the great killing facilities that flanked the ramp. No. 2 was dismantled and destroyed, with the other three facilities, in late November 1944, just nineteen months after it went "on line."

The question is frequently asked: How could so many have gone passively to their deaths? The calm expressions of the victims in this photograph provide the basic answer: Even as they pass directly between killing centers No. 1 and No. 2, in their last hour on earth, they still do not know the truth. By placing them against this backdrop, the photographer shows that he knows.

After Delousing

Nach der Entlausung

These men await further processing after their trip through the sauna and the issuing of underwear. They have been allowed to keep only belts and, sometimes, shoes. **In Man's Search for Meaning,** *Viktor Frankl writes of his initiation:*

"We waited in a shed which seemed to be the anteroom to the disinfecting chamber. SS men appeared and spread out blankets into which we had to throw all our possessions, all our watches and jewelry. There were still naive prisoners among us who asked, to the amusement of the more seasoned ones who were there as helpers, if they could not keep a wedding ring, a medal or a good luck piece. No one could yet grasp the fact that everything would be taken away.

"While we were waiting for the shower, our nakedness was brought home to us: we really had nothing now except our bare bodies—even minus hair; all we possessed, literally, was our naked existence."

The first two huts in each camp section were washrooms and toilets. Running water dripped out of holes in a pipe and toilets were simply a long line of holes in a board over a trough. Regardless of need, prisoners had only a standard thirty seconds on the toilet. They risked a beating by taking longer or by sneaking back. Ben Edelbaum, "caught" at the wrong time, was beaten so that his arms became swollen. "In my fifteen-year-old mind," he writes, "I kept wondering whether [they] would stop hurting and heal before I was put to death in the gas chambers. I also kept thinking how ridiculous it was to think that way in the first place. I mean, what difference did it make whether I was all right or not before going to my death?"

128

The man at front left has been seen previously, in photo 51, wearing a doctor's armband. Since he is now in the men's hospital compound—these are the only photos known to have been taken on the premises—it is probable that others shown here are also doctors or others working in the hospital huts. Several of the men seem too old to have been selected for work, and it is probably only their skills that have saved them from gassing.

The hospital huts served more to isolate sick patients than to make them well. "Patients" were crowded together in one another's filth, discharges from those on upper bunks dripping onto those lower down. Rags were used for bandages. Medicines were so hard to come by that a prisoner-doctor named Otto Wolken once tied an aspirin to a string and instructed those patients with low fever to "lick it once" and those with high fever "twice." By 1944 the situation was somewhat better, but this was due mainly to efforts of prisoner-doctors to acquire supplies brought by their Hungarian colleagues.

It may seem a paradox that any medical facilities at all should be provided for Jewish prisoners in a place designed specifically for their extinction, but this was in keeping with the Nazi attempt to put a veneer of normalcy on the place. Hospital huts contributed to the masquerade. In any case, these places were, despite the selfless efforts of the captive doctors and nurses, hardly more than a way station to the killing facilities. Prisoners who knew about the frequent selections conducted there would do anything not to be sent to the hospital.

129

130

131

132

"I had two photographs with me, one of my daughters and the other of my nephew on crutches. I realized that during the search they would take my precious souvenirs from me, so I tore out the heads and placed the scraps under my tongue. We had a piece of bread left, and my sister-in-law had a two-dollar bill. She wanted to throw the bill away, but I told her not to. I took it from her, folded it up, and concealed it in the bread...

"A group of Slovakian girls stood at the entrance to the bath-house, holding scissors and razor blades.... From afar we could see the girls making careful body checks, poking around in women's mouths and examining the soles of their feet, in case anyone had attached paper money to them. One of them cut the hair off our heads, a second shaved the hair from our bodies while a third held a painter's brush, which she dipped in some kind of liquid and daubed the shaven parts of our bodies. Then we were told to dip our shoes in a stinking black liquid and to leave by the back door.

"The search did not take long; after all, there are not many places to conceal things on naked bodies. Soon it was my turn. First they took the piece of bread from me, broke it in half and found the two-dollar bill inside. The girl who was doing the search took the bill and with a rapid movement hid it beneath her apron. With that, she concluded her search...and then [I was] hastily pushed forward."

And the Sun Kept Shining
by Bertha Ferderber-Salz

The puddle of water at right and the pile of stones at left are emblematic of life in the women's camp, B I. Drainage was a disastrous problem throughout the camp and in particular here on the south side of the ramp. Water covered the roads, the paths and even the floors of the huts. Erich Kulka, coming here on a work detail in November 1942, saw women everywhere too weak to pull their feet out of the "slimy earth," slowly dying. Even for a man well hardened to Dantesque scenes of Auschwitz life, Kulka found this women's camp to be too much. He could work there only two hours at a time before having to flee from these "visions of death."

Stones were a tool for punishment. Women were commonly ordered to carry a pile of stones back and forth between two places until they were exhausted. Then they could be declared fodder for the gas chambers. As another punishment, women were forced to kneel bare-kneed on gravel, holding stones in their outstretched hands. If one dropped, as it inevitably did, the women were beaten.

135

136

At least one, and possibly two, of the women in the group in photo 137 appear to be pregnant. As long as the condition wasn't too noticeable on the platform—and, bundled under coats, it was easy to miss—a pregnant woman could still be spared for work. But as soon as a living child was born, it and the mother were usually sent directly to the gas chamber. However, in a weird twist of the Nazi mind, as reported by an infirmary nurse named Olga Lengyel, the mother could be spared if the child was stillborn. Lengyel and her hapless colleagues, consequently, made a decision to kill babies upon birth and report that they were stillborn.

"The only meager consolation," she writes in **Five Chimneys**, "is that by these murders we saved the mothers... Yet I try in vain to make my conscience acquit me. I still see the infants issuing from their mothers. I can feel their warm little bodies as I held them. I marvel to what depths these Germans made us descend!"

119

These young women wear, in lieu of stripes, the coarse gray cloth issued to female slaves. Under the watchful eye of the SS man to the right of their column, they are entering B I, on the south side of the ramp. Many of them looked dazed and disbelieving, as well they might after disinfection at the sauna. They were deeply humiliated—more so than the men—at being forced to strip before leering, scornful SS guards. Until then, few of them had shown so much as a kneecap in public. Rose Moskowitz, from Bilke, arriving at the sauna, remembers her own shock at seeing two young brothers from a very religious family who had been her neighbors back home. They had been forced to work at the sauna. Suddenly they came face to face with their own two sisters, both naked except that one wore a sanitary belt. Mrs. Moskowitz still remembers how the two boys blanched and looked down in utter dismay.

121

Assignment to Labor Camp

Einweisung ins Arbeitslager

These women, in the charge of the stout Kapo at left, have just come from the sauna. They wear the ragtag clothing of those who went before them. Their youth indicates they have survived a selection, and their decent shoes—a rarity at Birkenau—suggest they will be shipped shortly to other labor camps. When Tzipora Halivni's outbound transport was abruptly delayed for days, the SS made the women give back their shoes, lest they be dirtied by excreta in the horrendously crowded holding huts.

140

The three-chimneyed building at right is the kitchen of the Hungarian women's camp. Couriers were dispatched to the kitchen from each hut three times a day to pick up rations— ersatz coffee in the morning, soup at noon, bread with margarine or sugar-beet jam and, on occasion, a bit of sausage in the evening. Magda Szabo, a Transylvanian deportee who worked in this kitchen, has described the soup as follows: "A few potatoes with a bit of margarine in a 75-gallon vat. We had to pour something in and stir, a sort of flour with a nasty taste. It was the camp-soup flavor."

Olga Lengyel, who was quartered in hut 27, reports that from the soup were fished "buttons, tufts of hair, rags, tin cans, keys and even mice." One day somebody even found a "tiny metal sewing kit, containing thread and an assortment of needles!" Only one red enameled bowl was available for each twenty persons in Lengyel's hut. So a system was devised by which a given number of gulps was allotted to each woman under the "glaring eyes" of her neighbors. "Jealously they counted every mouthful and watched the slightest movement of her Adams apple" until her share was consumed. In this fashion the bowl was passed along nineteen times until it was empty.

In the photo at right, the forest of fence stanchions behind the guard tower formed the northeast corner of camp B IIc and the northwest corner of the adjoining camp B IIb, known as the Czech family camp. This camp held Jews deported from the "show" ghetto at Theresienstadt. Alone among Jews at Auschwitz, they were permitted to live as families under comparatively good conditions, including the right to receive food parcels from abroad. As at Theresienstadt, they were even able to establish schools in the camp. But it was all for naught. On March 7, 1944, 3,800 men, women and children from the Czech family camp were delivered to killing facilities No. 1 and No. 2. At the last moment, from within the gas chamber itself, arose the strains of the Czech national anthem and then the Jewish anthem, "Hatikvah." The Czech family camp ceased to exist with a second gassing on July 12, 1944.

147

"We stood there, shivering, trembling, cropped and ragged. And only then did we look at each other. Not even the closest relatives were recognizable. Mothers didn't know their daughters, girls didn't recognize their sisters. Some of us had the hair on our heads shaved in stripes, others were completely bald, and others were left with tiny, isolated wisps. Ears stood out abnormally, and round or long-shaped heads were grotesquely prominent. Even what had been the most intelligent of faces seemed now to have taken on imbecilic expressions. Fortunately, we couldn't see ourselves, but some, looking at their companions, burst into hysterical laughter or uncontrollable weeping....

"It seemed to me for a moment that thousands of beggars [dressed in] the most outlandish rags had gathered together at a fancy-dress ball! Here they were, tiny women holding up the trains of their evening dresses, as our grandmothers did; or big fat women in garments split in two which cut tightly in their buttocks....

"On the other side of the wire fence, hundreds of other women were standing exactly like ourselves, divested of all human semblance. They called to us: "Are any of you from Kassa or Ujheli? When did you come?" We didn't dare reply, because a sound from us would have meant being whipped by the SS or by the Kapos as they counted us....

"At last we were lined up in military order—200 baldheaded, naked prisoners. The silence was broken only by the rasping voice of an SS man who kept shouting, 'Jewish swine! Schweinhund! Jewish whores!'"

Reska Weiss, Journey Through Hell

Personal Effects

Effekten

The three elements of SS policy toward Jews at Birkenau were theft, enslavement and murder. The catchword covering all phases of the first element was "Canada." It referred to the prisoner brigade (seen in earlier photographs) that removed the property of the deportees from the ramp, to the area of warehouses where the goods were delivered, and to the staff which processed them there.

By 1944 "Canada" had been removed entirely to a complex of thirty huts at the west end of Birkenau. With the advent of the Hungarian deportations, the prisoner staff rose to nearly a thousand. Trainloads of goods were regularly shipped back to the Reich. And yet, as these photos indicate, the big new "Canada" was still filled to overflowing. The take from the Hungarian deportees exceeded all that had been stolen before.

The plunder included figs and olives from the Greek transports, sardines and cheese from Holland, Hungarian salamis, chocolate from Belgium, brandy, tobacco and perfume from France. Hidden away—though not from the practiced eye and hand of the "Canada" searchers—were money, jewels, gold and silver.

This work was assigned almost exclusively to Jews, who routinely handled riches which, paradoxically, their SS overseers were forbidden to touch. This work was reserved for them, according to the Birkenau historian Tzipora Hager Halivni, precisely because unlike the SS or even the non-Jewish prisoners, the Jews alone were considered to be irrevocably doomed and so were thought to have the least to gain by dipping into the "Canada" riches.

Despite all precautions and threats, however, the SS overseers as well as the prisoners managed to skim from the "Canada" abundance. Auschwitz was ruined, Commandant Höss complains in his memoirs, by "Jewish gold." But even his own wife, according to testimony given by the family gardener, was sending packages of "Canada" booty back to her relatives in the Reich.

155

To facilitate "quick delivery," the deported families were instructed to print their names in large block letters on their luggage, as has been done on the trunk at left in photo 156. A woman from Bilke, arriving at Birkenau on the Sabbath with one suitcase still unmarked, asked the sexton of the town synagogue, David Reisman, if she could violate the commandment to rest on this day by writing on her suitcase. After some contemplation, here under the shadow of the crematoria chimneys, he advised her that she should not.

Rudolf Vrba, a Czech Jew who was one of the very few to eventually escape from Birkenau, claimed that he learned more about the "real purpose" of the camp during his first week working in "Canada" than in the three months since he had arrived. What most appalled him was not the "sadism or the brutality or the sporadic deaths" he said in I Cannot Forgive, *but the "cold-blooded commercialism of the place":*

"Slowly the bags and the clothes and the food and the sad, smiling photographs became people to me; the prams became babies and the heaps of carefully segregated little shoes became children, like my cousin, Lici, in Topolcany."

Luggage so painstakingly packed is split open as soon as it is dumped off the trucks here at "Canada." Since the huts were always full, the goods had to be sorted here on the sodden ground.

162

"We…found ourselves near a building to the right of which was a large mound about the size of a two-story building. As we neared the mound we saw it was made entirely of shoes: women's shoes, children's shoes, beautiful shoes, ugly shoes—shoes wherever the eye rested. And this was the rise we had mistaken for a hill!"

Reska Weiss, Journey Through Hell

The intimacy of murder and theft at Birkenau is emphasized in photo 167. These women of "Canada," working amid the heaps of water vessels, had only to look through the fence at right to see, on the other side, the grove where Jews waited to be taken into killing facility No. 3.

"Then I saw the women. Real women, not the terrible, sexless skeletons whose bodies stank and whose hearts were dead.... These were young, well-dressed girls with firm ripe figures and faces made beautiful by health alone. They were bustling everywhere, running to and fro with bundles of clothes and parcels, watched by even healthier, even more elegant woman kapos."

Rudolf Vrba, on this first day working in "Canada." From I Cannot Forgive.

Despite three separate searches carried out by "dead drunk" SS men at the end of the working day, Halina Birenbaum writes in Hope Is the Last to Die *that she always managed to bring something back to her fellow prisoners who did not have the luck to work in "Canada." "I vied with the others in this respect. So many things, pillaged from our murdered brothers, the Jewish people from Hungary, were going to waste under-foot that—or so it seemed to me—it would rescue the entire camp from the torments of starvation, illness and dirt. How, then, was it possible to come back empty-handed from Canada?*

"Every day I put on a new pair of shoes at work, came back wearing them and gave them to comrades in the camp; in the morning I went to work in old, shabby and rotten wooden clogs which I threw into the trashcan in Canada. . . . I would bring back pieces of scented soap or fine silken underwear in shoes that were too big, for they did not make us take our shoes off during checks. We smuggled gloves, blouses, underwear on our stomachs, under the coarse striped camp chemise. I hid pieces of bread, cake, bacon under my own clothing as I held it during searches, and returned with a beating heart thus loaded."

170

Birkenau

This is the Birkenau—the birch grove. Here, amid the slender birches and pines at the northwestern corner of the camp, Jews who had walked the half mile from the ramp waited to be admitted to the killing facility. The SS would have preferred that there be no wait at all. But there remained the problem, never satisfactorily solved, of how to burn corpses as fast as the living people had been gassed. In the early days of the camp, before the construction of the four huge killing facilities, bodies had been buried. But then, in the spring of 1942, the ground began to heave and turn red. Decomposing bodies were actually bursting out of the earth. Teams of prisoners were dispatched to dig up the restless remains and burn them.

From the spring of 1943, the dead were burned in the four efficient new crematoria, but not fast enough. Anticipating that the work of the crematoria would fall even further behind during the upcoming Hungarian deportations, the camp command took steps in the early spring to augment their capacity.

Under the direction of Hauptscharführer Otto Moll, teams were put to work digging a series of long, wide trenches close by the killing facilities. Following gassing, the bodies were delivered here by wagon and stacked with alternating layers of firewood or flammable refuse. Since there were no fans as in the crematoria, the fires had to be constantly stoked. Moll designed a series of channels at the bottom of the pits into which the rendered fat would drop. The channels then slanted downward toward each end of the pit, where the fat was collected and poured back over the bodies as additional fuel.

While this conflagration was hidden by the depth of the pits, by camouflage fences and by the trees of the Birkenau, the smell and the pall in the air were noted well beyond the confines of the camp.

171

172

173

175

176

Apprehensive as they may be, these families still trusted that, following disinfection, they would be bound for the family camp. In cases where the SS suspected the people knew better, they dropped the charade. This was the case when selections were made from within the camp populace or among certain newly arriving groups which, because they had lived fairly near the camp, could not be fooled.

Such was the status of 2,000 Jews from the ghettos of nearby Sosnovitz and Bedzin, deported here in August 1943. On the dawn of their arrival, according to Filip Muller, they were driven through the camp at a run, shrieking and wailing, by a specially augmented SS force. Those who fell were killed at once. In the grove, the people were ordered tersely and without the usual blandishments to remove their clothing.

Suddenly, reports Muller, an "emaciated little man" began to recite the ancient prayer of contrition that begins 'bagadti' (we have sinned), 'gazalti' (we have wronged our fellow man), 'dibarti' (we have slandered)...The chant was taken up by all and began to ring through the grove. Muller was surprised to see that although the SS men kept checking their watches impatiently, they did not intervene.

The congregation in the grove concluded with the Kaddish, the prayer for the dead. Traditionally, it is said only by the surviving family, but knowing they were doomed, the people now said it for themselves: "Yiskadal veyiskadash, sh'mai rabah" (Magnified and sanctified be the name of the Holy One)...

As the people walked to the gas chamber, there was great weeping. But, writes Muller, "their tears were not tears of despair. These people were in a state of deep religious emotion. They had put themselves in God's hands."

178

179

180

"From between two lines formed by SS men they were herded into the nearby grove. And now their fate was finally sealed; for here, within the shadow of the crematorium and its three gas chambers, there was no escape.

"They were standing some hundred meters from the pits, their view blocked by a 3-meters high camouflage screen: a few SS guards, their rifles at the ready, were posted in front of the screen to prevent anyone from going too close and through the gaps stealing a glance at the inferno behind it....

"But the imagination of the people could not possibly envisage that the smoke clouding the sun, the huge fire raging behind the screen and the sickly smell polluting the air came from the burning of thousands of murdered human beings who, only a few hours earlier, had suffered the fate now awaiting them.... Every now and then, Hauptscharführer Moll put in an appearance, asking people to be patient and promising that soon they would be given something to drink....

Several of the people were so desperately thirsty that they crouched on the ground licking the dew-wet grass. When the long-promised drink failed to materialize the people began to grow restless, distressed above all by the piteous cries and entreaties of their children who were begging their mothers for just a few drops of water....This pre-programmed suffering was deliberately aimed at paralyzing the ability to notice things and the will to resist in order to allow the giant machinery of murder to run smoothly and at full speed."

From an account of the arrival of
Hungarian Jews in this June of 1944.

Visible in the background are warehouse huts of "Canada."
Ten of the thirty huts directly bordered this grove and also kill-
ing facility No. 4 itself. The view from the other direction can be
seen at the right of photo 185.

184

The child at the center of the picture on the right is among the youngest in these photographs to wear the yellow star. As of April 5, 1944, the star had to appear on the left breast of all Hungarian Jews over the age of six years. Filip Muller, forced with other prisoners to clean out a changing room after a gassing, remembers how the clothing left behind was strewn over the concrete floor, the "Stars of David like a drift of yellow flowers."

185

This group, coming from the ramp, has just turned off the upper end of the main camp road. They are about to enter the gate of killing facility No. 1. Though some people manage calm faces and even brave smiles in other photos, here they are gone.

*Soon after the Hungarian deportations began, a bag of post-
cards from the victims was delivered to the Jewish Council in
Budapest. The deportees claimed, in their own handwriting, to
be "well" and "working." The cards were all datelined "Waldsee," which the Nazis said was a work camp in Germany. But a
council member, Philipp von Freudiger, came across a card with
an erasure. "The word Waldsee had been rubbed out," Freudiger testified on May 25, 1961, at the trial of Adolf Eichmann
in Jerusalem. "As a textile manufacturer, I always kept a magnifying glass handy on my desk, and I noticed the letters
"—itz" were visible...I took the postcard to Krumey (an Eichmann lieutenant) and said: 'Our people are in Auschwitz, not
in Waldsee.' He said, 'How can you say such a thing?' I gave
him the postcard and the magnifying glass and said: 'Please
take a look.' He examined it and said, 'Freudiger, I know you
are a sensible man—you should not be too observant.' Then the
postcards stopped coming—in fact, there were no people to
write those postcards any more."*

187

"On behalf of the camp administration I bid you welcome. This is not a holiday resort but a labor camp. Just as our soldiers risk their lives at the front to gain victory for the Third Reich, you will have to work here for the welfare of a new Europe. How you tackle this task is entirely up to you. The chance is there for every one of you. We shall look after your health, and we shall also offer you well-paid work. After the war we shall assess everyone according to his merits and treat him accordingly.

"Now, would you please all get undressed. Hang your clothes on the hooks we have provided and please remember your number [of the hook]. When you've had your bath there will be a bowl of soup and coffee or tea for all. Oh yes, before I forget, after your bath, please have ready your certificates, diplomas, school reports and any other documents so that we can employ everybody according to his or her training and ability.

"Would diabetics who are not allowed sugar report to staff on duty after their baths."

—Speech given in the dressing room at the portals of the gas chamber by Obersturmführer Hössler to a group of Greek Jews, as paraphrased by Sonderkommando member Filip Muller

188